Believe in Promises
and
Enjoy the ride !!
Sincerely
Lucian + Lori
Promise March
10/27/18

THE LONG RIDE

Publisher's Cataloguing-in-Publication Data

Spataro Jr., Lucian
The Long Ride: The Record-Setting Journey by Horse Across the American Landscape

ISBN-13: 978-0-9835019-0-9

BISAC: NATURE | Environmental Conservation & Protection

For information contact Green Rider LLC, Scottsdale, AZ | info@thelongride.com

Edited by Claire Gerus, Claire Gerus Literary Agency, Tucson, AZ

Interior and Cover Design by Bill Greaves, Concept West, Cave Creek, AZ

Typesetting by 1106 Design, Phoenix, AZ

Printed in China by Everbest through Four Colour Print Group, Louisville, KY

Mixed Sources
Product group from well-managed forests, and other controlled sources
www.fsc.org Cert no. SGS-COC-003563
© 1996 Forest Stewardship Council
FSC

THE
LONG
RIDE

Please visit www.thelongride.com for further information.

IMAGE CREDITS

Joan Andrew – Illustrations, p.37, p.65, p.71, p.117 and p.161
Courtesy of Athens County Historical Society and Museum – p.177
Courtesy A/P Wide World Photos – p.38
Victoria Bellerose – p.58 and p.159, courtesy of Victoria Bellerose by permission of Loudon Times Mirror
Charles E. Brooks – Inside back flap, p. vii and p.193
Melanie Coward – p.41 and p.43
Christy Cumberworth – p.195
Equis/Tim Davis – p.167, top right insert
Dan Duncan p.12 and p.204
Doug Engle – p.139, top right
Easycare Inc. – p.30 and p.52
Randall Gingrich – p.14
JGI Photo Library – p.5
Kevin Green – p.134 and p.135
J.P. Isner – p.144, bottom, p.147 insets provided by J.P. Isner, p.149 provided by J.P. Isner
Ohio University Photo Archive – p.33 and p.137
Ohio Valley Environmental Coalition – p.187
Peggy Larson – p.197, center
Patriot News/Bob Levy – p.140
Char Magaro – p.169, p.172, p.173 and p.175
Kathy Nichols – p.66 and p.67
Susanne Page – p.8, p.9, p.10, p.11, p.24 and p.25, top
Molly Zehr Palmer – p.166
Rainforest Action Network – p.15, p.17, p.18, p.25, p.28, bottom and p.30
Rosemary Renteria and Angie Wood – Map, p.48
Louise Serpa – p.75
Steve Shaluta – p.147 main shot provided by Steve Shaluta, p.151, p.153 and p.155
Bob and Bea Shepard – Contents page, p.vi, p.viii, p.7, p.56, p.59, p.77, p.80, p.81, p.88, top, p.89, p.91, p.92, p.99, p.103, p.109, p.111, p.115, p.123, p.129, inset, p.164, p.165, p.167, p.171 and p.174
Betsy Stanton – p.127
Cie Stroud – p.4, p.26, p.121, p.126, bottom, p.129, top, p.139, p.143, and p.144, top
Suzan Victoria – Front cover, title page, p.viii, p.27, p.34, p.35, p.45, p.48, p.49, p.55, and p.145
Walter Woodcock – Illustration, p.54

Every effort has been made to trace copyright holders. If any unintended omissions have been made, Green Rider LLC would be pleased to add an appropriate acknowledgment in future editions.

THE LONG RIDE

The Record-Setting Journey by Horse Across the American Landscape

Lucian Spataro Jr., Ph.D.

GREEN RIDER LLC

Scottsdale | Arizona

For Bazy Tankersly and the horses AM Sweet William, AM March Along, and AM Sea Ruler,
my wife Lori, and my parents Lucian Sr. and Dorothy Spataro,
and the thousands and thousands of people we met along the way who supported our efforts
and inspired us to "carry this message" and keep on riding.

THE LONG RIDE
TABLE OF CONTENTS

ACKNOWLEDGMENTS

You don't often get a chance in life to "do good" by doing what you love. But in 1989, I did get that chance as I had the opportunity to combine my passion for horses and the environment in the "Ride Across America." Now 20 plus years later, we have arrived at a very important juncture as our human population continues past seven billion people and our footprint is growing larger every day; if we continue to move forward as we are now, we will most certainly find ourselves at an environmental precipice.

As we look over the edge, we can see very clearly the impact and we can no longer ignore the fact that our actions are fundamentally altering the planet and those natural systems that support life, as we know it. It is a scary realization but one that represents at the same time a unique and unparalleled opportunity to "right the wrongs" and rally the global community around a common cause that is inherently more important that anything we will ever do as humans past, present, or future. Our future and that of generations to come is shaped today by our actions and it is seems crazy to imagine that as intelligent as we are that we are incapable of making a conscious decision to act in consensus and change our behavior and rise to this challenge.

As I sit here today writing these words, it is as clear today as it was 20 years ago why we did the ride and why I am writing this second book. Each of us has a part to play and I am playing my part. I am hoping that these words and this book will motivate others to make a similar choice and we can share this moment and ride this road together.

My purpose in writing this second book was, first and foremost, to thank the many people who helped us achieve our objectives, while at the same time, keeping these environmental issues on the front burner. I met many people along the way who, like me, are trying to effect a positive change in their own way and at their own pace. I have found that everyone really can and does make a difference.

With this in mind, I would like to thank the horses: AM Sweet William, AM March Along and AM Sea Ruler, as well as my teammates, Bea and Bob Shepard and Joyce and Brad Braden, whose perseverance and commitment for the duration was constant. Our support team: Francesca Vietor, Dave Trexler, and Dr. Hancock, were instrumental in getting us through some of the rougher stretches.

Special thanks goes to Mrs. Bazy Tankersley, who, when I needed credibility early in the organizational phase, helped me by getting on board early in the event. Her commitment and belief in our team and this event anchored us and quieted the naysayers. She often said, "In this race, to finish is to win." Bazy supported us without question, and buoyed our spirits at every turn and from every perspective.

I also want to thank Randall Hayes, Ted Danson, and Leslie Barclay, who unwaveringly supported our efforts and were always available to help us when needed. In the overall scheme of things, these people were instrumental to the success of our ride.

After the ride was over, I convinced myself to write the first book, *Ride Across America*. I was a new author and for such an undertaking, I needed lots of help. I got most of the help from people who were attracted to this project for environmental reasons.

Today, twenty-plus years later, I am writing the second book, *The Long Ride*.

I want to thank Claire Gerus, who helped me recall important aspects of the ride that were buried memories for all these years, or were missing from the original manuscript. As Claire and I collaborated chapter by chapter, month after month, her gentle prodding, skillful editing and ongoing feedback allowed me to rethink my approach and create this second book.

I would also like to thank Bill Greaves, my designer, who really brought the pages to life with graphics and art direction, and to Marie Baranowski for the last minute proofreading.

Thanks, too, to Karl Knelson, who made it all work on the website.

I would also like to thank my father, Lucian Spataro Sr., who provided me with a place to hide while writing the first book, and offered a second set of eyes and constructive criticism for the second book.

I am grateful to my mother, Dorothy Spataro, who had the unenviable task of keeping my personal life in order while I was on the ride, and who provided encouragement along the way. Both my parents instilled in me at an early age that above all, when you do what is right you can't be wrong, so do what you think is right—regardless of the challenges it may present.

Most importantly, I must thank my wife, Lori, whose moral support and multi-tasking ability during the two years that it took to write this book, assemble the photos, and complete the website, gave me time and space. She helped me juggle responsibilities at home and at work so I could finish the book and keep all the balls in the air while remaining sane. Lori, you never doubted me and always supported me. You understood why I was doing this even though others did not—and for that, I will be eternally grateful.

Without these people and these horses, the ride and this book would not have been possible. All, in their own way, helped bring this ride to life. Life is really about how we choose to travel the road we travel, and with whom. Ultimately, this is what this book is all about— memories of a place in time when we were doing the "right thing." So saddle up, I hope you enjoy this ride.

Lucian Spataro Jr., Ph.D.

THE LONG RIDE
STATISTICS

ABOVE TOP Lucian and March Along on a training ride in Tucson, Arizona.

ABOVE Brad and Sweet William take a quick photo before saddling up in northern Arizona.

Dates
May 19, 1989 to October 15, 1989. 150 days coast-to-coast

Distance
2,963 miles. 19.75 miles per day on average

Number of States
13 states, plus the District of Columbia

Temperature Range
130 degrees in the shade in Twenty Nine Palms, California, and 15 degrees in Maryland

Number of Permits Required to Cross the U.S. by Horse
Sixty seven permits required

Number of Horses
Three horses: AM Sweet William (Willy), AM Sea Ruler (Ruler), and AM March Along (March)

Distance for Each Horse
Willy 1,440 miles; Ruler 912 miles; March 611 miles

Number of Riders
One rider, Lucian Spataro Jr.

Rider's Weight
165 lbs in May and 143 lbs in October

Training Time and Distance Before the Ride
4 Months (January–May, 1989). 1,800 miles on all three horses

Total Distance and Time Including Training
4,763 miles in 9 months (January–October 15, 1989). 17.6 miles per day average for nine months

THE LONG RIDE

WINDOW
ROCK, AZ

FLAGSTAFF, AZ

GALLUP, NM

SANTA
ROSA, NM

LOS ANGELES, CA

HUNTINGTON
BEACH

ALBUQUERQUE, NM

LAKE HAVASU, AZ

AMARILLO, TX

MAP OF
THE LONG RIDE

MAY 19 TO OCTOBER 15, 1989

CHESAPEAKE BEACH

GRAFTON, WV

WINCHESTER, VA

ATHENS, OH

SELVIN, IN

PARKERSBURG, WV

COVINGTON, KY

WASHINGTON, DC

NEW
ALBANY, IN

MADISON, IN

FARMINGTON, MO

JOPLIN, MO

WEST
FRANKFURT, IL

TULSA, OK

SPRINGFIELD, MO

OKLAHOMA
CITY, OK

CORDELL, OK

FOREWORD

ABOVE Lucian and March Along riding east into the early morning fog, southern Ohio.

BELOW Rainforests which serve as home to millions of indigenous species previously blanketed 14 percent of the planet but today cover less than 6 percent, and the rate of deforestation is accelerating. Through the process of photosynthesis, rainforests serve as a carbon sink by absorbing carbon dioxide and producing at the same time almost a third of the oxygen on the planet.

OPPOSITE Jane Goodall, Founder of The Jane Goodall Institute.

Twenty years ago Lucian Spataro rode on horseback 2,963 miles across America. He did this because he felt so strongly that all was not right with our world, and he wanted to draw attention to the way in which we humans were destroying our environment. Stopping along the way he discussed the situation with the people he met. Many listened to him because they were fascinated by the man and his horses, then because they were fascinated, and often shocked, by what he was telling them. In the same way, people often come to my talks because they are fascinated by what they know of my life with the chimpanzees, then become concerned as I speak about the harm we are inflicting on Planet Earth.

Lucian's journey was not an easy one. The book describes, often with humor, the many hardships he—and his horses—endured along the way. We empathize, we marvel, at the journey itself. And then we start to think about the reason why he embarked on such a crazy trek. And we realize that, indeed, all is not well with our world.

Sadly the world is, in many ways, in an even worse situation than it was 20 years ago when Lucian and his horses plodded across a continent. There are more human

beings on the planet and less animal and plant species. Unimaginably vast areas of forest have been destroyed, wetlands drained, grasslands turned to dust. Chemical fertilizers, pesticides, preservatives and so on contaminate and poison land, water and air. Millions of people have no easy access to fresh water, millions die of hunger and disease. War and violence, intolerance, hatred and fear stalk the land. Yet we can turn this around if we will but roll up our sleeves and take action to put things right—in our own small way, in our own neck of the woods.

This is why it is so important that Lucian's story and his message is brought to a wider audience in this revised book. You will be filled with admiration for this man, and absorbed by his story of adventure and determination. You will also be left with a sense of urgency and the understanding that you, too, can make a difference, make this a better world for all living things.

Jane Goodall Ph.D., DBE

Founder—The Jane Goodall Institute

and UN Messenger of Peace

www.janegoodall.org

BELOW The rainforest canopy by some estimates is home to 50 percent of all plant and animal species, suggesting that perhaps half of all life on Earth could be found here. As long ago as 1917, naturalist William Beebe declared that "another continent of life remains to be discovered, not upon the Earth, but one to two hundred feet above it, extending over thousands of square miles."

OPPOSITE "It is known that when people find themselves in a survival situation, 5 percent of the people will do the wrong thing, 5 percent will do the right thing, and 90 percent will do nothing at all – but in a many cases they all survive, thanks generally to those who did the right thing. The U.S. with 5 percent of the world's population has a footprint that is more impactful than 80 percent of the rest of the people on the planet. Let's be that 5 percent that does the right thing, and if we do, we will be well on our way to turning this situation around." —Lucian Spataro Jr.

INTRODUCTION

I first met Lucian Spataro at an Up With People event in Tucson. This was after receiving his FedEx package, handwritten note, and a follow-up phone call the next day. He was and continues to be a whirlwind of passion and persistence about environmental preservation.

In our first meeting, he demonstrated to me the level of commitment required to take on a project of this magnitude, meet his objectives as outlined, and actually complete his mission. He spoke in detail about the planning and training that would be required. Lucian also conveyed a sense of urgency when talking about the environmental message he would bring to citizens in both small and large communities across the country.

When he described to me how our Arabian horses would draw people into the excitement of the ride and forge a strong connection with them, his ideas struck a chord in me. His message was spot on, unique and very appealing—exactly the kind of event that would garner the attention needed to begin a national dialogue on this very important issue.

ABOVE Lucian and Bazy Tankersley collaborating on the Black Stallion Project, Al-Marah Arabians, November, 2005.

BELOW A field of mares and foals at Al-Marah.

OPPOSITE Mommies and their babies relaxing in the shade of a cottonwood tree at Al-Marah.

That message—so powerfully conveyed during the ride—is even more relevant today as he brings his remarkable story to a much larger audience in his second book, *The Long Ride*. This was no leisurely stroll across the U.S. for a few days. Instead, it was a grueling event for both horses and humans. *The Long Ride* is a story of persistence and determination against long odds. Lucian's recounting is exciting, and the message is even more important today as our environmental systems face increasing odds against survival. As you read this story, you will see how we all play a role, and that every one of us can make a difference.

Bazy Tankersley
Owner, Al-Marah Arabians

BELOW Kicking up their heels, the Arabians of Al-Marah.

OPPOSITE A foal sharing a quiet moment with mom.

PREFACE

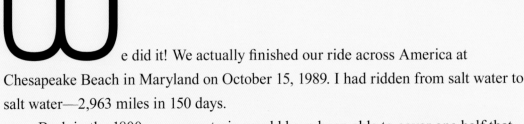

We did it! We actually finished our ride across America at Chesapeake Beach in Maryland on October 15, 1989. I had ridden from salt water to salt water—2,963 miles in 150 days.

Back in the 1800s, a wagon train would have been able to cover one half that distance from St. Louis to California in about 180 days. More recently, in the 1970s, a young woman rode three horses consecutively to complete a coast-to-coast ride in 300 days, or 10 months.

By present-day standards, a car traveling 60 miles an hour can cover the same distance I covered by horseback—2,963 miles—in about 50 hours. Our ride took 3,600 hours coast to coast at a speed of about one mile every sixteen minutes.

When we were in the desert, we could always see our destination—the horizon—in the distance. We always knew that it would take two weeks from one horizon to the next. But a plane flying coast to coast can cover this same distance in a mere five and a half hours.

So you can see how far technology has brought us. And yet, over the past 70 years, we have laid the foundation for most of the environmental problems that we now face.

People asked us many questions along the way as we rode across America. But the three questions they asked most often were:

1. "Why are you doing this?"
2. "Is it worth the effort?"
3. "Can we still save the environment?"

Following were my answers.

ABOVE Lucian and Sweet William sharing some carrot cake on Willy's 29th birthday, October 21, 2010, at Redington Ranch, Tucson, Arizona.

OPPOSITE "Hey guys, the camera is over here." Lucian trying to organize Sea Ruler and March Along for a photo opportunity in Missouri.

QUESTION ONE: *Why Are You Doing This?*

The simple answer was: We did it to draw attention to the plight of the rainforests. Someone once told me that a person cannot avoid doing what he is meant to do at the time he is meant to do it. I know that we were meant to take this ride at exactly that moment in time.

Back in 1988, the United States experienced a frightening drought. To me, this was a sign that the destruction of rainforests in remote parts of the world was starting to affect the climate here, as well as elsewhere across the globe. I wanted to do something about it, as did many others, especially environmental groups like the Rainforest Action Network (RAN). So I got together with RAN reps and we talked it through and began to plan the ride, with RAN as one of the sponsors. It seemed an event like this could bring attention to the forest preservation issue, and maybe even spark a grassroots campaign to save it.

But there were other reasons why we chose to hold this particular event. I'd always wanted to ride a horse across America, and welcomed the physical and mental challenge for myself and my teammates. And of course, there was the opportunity to set a record.

Then, once we got started, we couldn't quit, so even when the going got tough, we persevered. We did this for the people who had backed us and helped us plan and kept us going. But we also did it for the many people we met along the way. We had made a commitment to them to complete our mission, so not finishing the ride wasn't even on the table.

QUESTION TWO: *Is It Worth the Effort?*

As we began the event our objectives, in order of priority, were:
1. to complete the ride and establish a new record,
2. to talk to as many people as possible along the way about the rainforest issue,
3. to raise as much money as possible for the Rainforest Action Network.

We felt the horses and the event itself would attract attention and introduce people to this very important issue. And it worked! We personally spoke to about 20,000 people (about 150 a day) as we rode across the United States and introduced the issue to four or five million others through local and national magazine articles, radio and television.

While some people couldn't immediately relate to an issue that seemed so far away, everyone could relate to our commitment. Our example brought home a very strong message, and we offered people an opportunity to get involved in this critical environmental issue, and therein, I believe, lay our real success.

And, finally, we were able to raise quite a lot of money for the Rainforest Action Network. When we started the ride, we wanted to bring attention to this issue and to help RAN grow its membership base. As we spoke to more than 20,000 people directly and

BELOW and OPPOSITE Slash and Burn clearing of the rainforest for subsistence farming, cattle ranching, and the production of charcoal for cooking contributes to almost 30 percent of the carbon that is released into the atmosphere. With this increase in carbon dioxide we are actually altering the composition of the earth's atmosphere and trapping radiation that would normally escape and for this reason, the planet is warming.

calculated that media coverage put this issue in front of another 5 million people, we knew we had achieved our objective.

Now, in 2010, RAN can count over 15,000 supporters worldwide and is still growing. Today the organization works with more than 35 groups in 12 countries on environmental issues.

QUESTION THREE: *Can We Still Save The Environment?*

I had to really think about this before answering this question. Ultimately, I think the answer is "yes, we can." I firmly believe we still have the ability to do so, and that it will happen in this decade. But even if we aren't completely successful, we have a moral obligation to try. We have no right to give up a future for coming generations, and we have everything to gain by trying our best.

For me, the challenge is to learn how I can help with this effort. I know that we human beings must change our behavior, and that means changing our attitude toward our planet and its other inhabitants worldwide. Clearly, we need to understand the impact our actions have on all aspects of this ecosystem.

In my ride across America, I learned firsthand about many environmental problems as we clopped along, exposed to many actual issues along the route. Onlookers tended to talk about local environmental problems, so for them, the rainforest was of less interest than the challenges they were facing in their daily lives.

In some ways, it was more difficult to cross America by horseback in 1989 than it had been in 1889! In those days, there was no need to cross highways, negotiate bridges and organize permits. In those days, too, there weren't the same problems of consumption, waste, and environmental damage as there were in 1989.

On the ride, I often thought about how this had all gone out of control, and wondered what we could do to get everything back on track again. The place to start, of course, was with balance. If we alter one or more aspects of nature's normal ecosystem, the environment may be able to compensate by balancing it out. But if it's too far out of balance, the system may not be able to recover.

For example, one summer in Arizona, a farmer had an unusually good pecan crop. He was very excited because the year before he'd had a very small harvest. But he also saw more birds in the orchard than in previous years and he was concerned that the birds might eat all the immature nuts. So whenever the farmer saw the birds, he got out his gun and shot as many as he could.

Several weeks went by, and when the farmer was ready to harvest the pecans, he found that the nuts were infested with insect larvae. Many of the birds the farmer had seen in the spring had been feeding on adult insects, but with no birds to feed on them, they had been able to lay many eggs. These soon hatched into larvae, which grew very quickly and eventually infested the whole orchard.

ABOVE The Pony Express, St. Louis to San Francisco; no fences, no highways and no permits required. Fifty horses and 15 riders at very high speed could make the ride in 10 days. A wagon train from St. Louis to California would make the trip in 180 days.

OPPOSITE and PAGE 18 The rainforest canopy is home to most of the biodiversity in these forests and also this canopy doubles as a shield from the hot sun while stimulating the release of moisture that fuels the rainforest fog that sits on top of these forests.

OPPOSITE "When the Red Red Robin Comes Bob Bob Bobin' Along" you know you are in the Midwest. The American Robin is a migratory songbird that is widely distributed throughout North America and whose diet consists of beetle grubs and caterpillars, fruits and berries.

The farmer did not understand that when the birds ate the adult insects, they were keeping the population down. Instead, he assumed that the birds were eating the immature nuts. Because the farmer did not understand that the birds helped him keep the balance in the orchard, he had altered a critical relationship. He upset the balance of nature in his orchard and, as a result, lost his harvest.

In other cases, the balance is not as obvious. For example, if we cut down rainforests in South America many thousands of miles away, we do not see the impact, but we can feel it. Many of the birds that live in the United States during the summer live in the rainforest in winter. If these birds have no safe place to go and no food to eat when they arrive, they will die.

This means we will lose these beautiful creatures. As the years go by, we will hear fewer and fewer songbirds in the summer. But we will lose more than songs. Songbirds eat insects. Without them, the insect population will grow. The farmer may use pesticides to control them, but some of these poisons may get into our food or into the food chain of animals that eat insects. So a chain of destruction begun many miles away will eventually have disastrous consequences here, and the rainforests may be gone before we even see those consequences.

After realizing that any change to nature can have unforeseen consequences elsewhere, we know that before we make a change, we must first study the possible outcomes. If left alone, nature tends to balance itself. As humans, we must try to respect this balance. If we must change the natural order, we should be very, very careful. The outcome is too critical for us to act before we know what the consequences will be.

CHAPTER ONE:
HOW IT ALL BEGAN

On several occasions before the ride, I had a recurring dream. It was the year 2031 and l was now in my 70s. In the dream, I found myself in a house that was very cold. Although the lights were on, the room felt dark, although I had enough light to read a book. Then, my grandson walked in. He seemed to enter the room through some type of vacuum transition chamber. It seemed as if each room was "purified" before someone could enter or exit.

My grandson had a magazine with him and he wanted to discuss an article with me. A look of concern—maybe anger—was on his face. I noticed that the magazine in his hands was *TIME,* and the article he was pointing to was titled, "We Lost the Ecosystem. How?"

The article took the reader through a chronology of environmental and economic decisions, both bad and good, spanning 80 years. It explained why these decisions were made—economic and political reasons that were fueled by a growing population and a throwaway society.

The article declared that in the 1980s, the environment became a trendy issue and many celebrities became involved. People worked very hard to bring attention to the issue and several even walked across the United States. Others circulated petitions, organized sit-ins and participated in protest marches.

One person even rode a horse across America.

The article then gave a detailed account of all the symptoms of environmental disease that were apparent to everyone: acid rain, global deforestation, ozone depletion, and so on.

My grandson then looked at me, not smiling, and asked, "When all of this was going on, what were you doing?"

ABOVE Lucian and his dog Skipper. Beagles are known for their strong sense of smell and their ability to track game and for this reason, Skipper was an able and willing partner and very good at playing the seek side of "hide and seek" with Lucian.

OPPOSITE A quiet little pond in southern Ohio, is the foundation upon which a set of interactions between animals and plants that live around this pond function to support a web of life that is in balance.

ABOVE TOP Sunday after church was a big day for riding. Lucian is shown bringing Tim in from the woods for a ride.

ABOVE Tim is saddled up and ready to go down into Dobson Hollow.

A Red Tailed Hawk in flight.

I replied: "I rode the horse."

He walked over to the window and looked outside. Then, very slowly, he turned back to me and said: "Is that all? Is that it?"

At that point, I arose from my chair and walked to the window to look outside. There I saw a crow sitting in a dead tree. It was springtime, about 1:00 p.m., just after lunch.

And it was dark outside.

───────────────────

My interest in the environment had its roots in my youth. My parents introduced me to the world of nature when I was very young, and even as a third-grader I understood that the world was operating under a kind of master plan. I was not, however, aware that this plan rested on a naturally balanced ecosystem. A naturally balanced ecosystem is a group of animals and plants within a unit that live or function together in natural balance. We humans are a part of this ecosystem.

Today, when I look back on my youth, my memories are of my days in Latourette's Forest, Essex Pond, and Dobson Hollow in southern Ohio. Dobson Hollow was a very deep valley about two miles from my home. It featured huge rock cliffs above, with a red-tailed hawk nest and a clear stream and meadows down below. It seemed that very few people went down into this hollow, but my friends and I loved exploring the streams, ponds and valleys.

There were animals everywhere: deer, hawk, quail, largemouth bass, frogs, fireflies and turtles. I had the unique opportunity to gain an appreciation for the natural world through these sometimes aimless wanderings and explorations. I would spend many hours and sometimes days on my horses, Buck and Tim, or hiking with friends through the area.

My beagle, Skipper, accompanied me on many of these trips. Our favorite game was, "I hide, you seek." I'd leave home and hike into the woods, sometimes several miles and try to disguise my trail. Then, I'd find a high vantage point—often a ridge—and watch my dog pick up my trail, following me through streams, over logs, from rock to rock and across wooden fences. I'd learned how to elude him by watching fox and rabbits as they were being trailed. (Rabbits always return in a complete circle home.)

I also learned a lot about patience and persistence, both from my dog and from these forest animals. We used to photograph deer from tree stands in the early morning as they were moving into the apple orchards, and through these childhood experiences, I became educated, fascinated and appreciative of the natural world.

I sense that today, children and adults rarely take advantage of, or are exposed to, these kinds of opportunities, and because of this children today do not feel a connection to the natural world. We have grown away from nature, thanks in large part to technology, that double-edged sword, with its computers and video games substituting for the appeal many children once found in nature. Without the most basic exposure, we will miss the vital connection we have with natural systems.

We as a society have isolated ourselves within our technology, and no longer feel the real cold or the rain or heat. Few of us question how or where the food we eat is produced. How many of us even know how it gets to our grocers? We need to rediscover nature and the fascination it held for many of us in years past.

Given all the above, I decided that now was the time to bring this awareness to the rest of America—by riding across it by horse.

Organizing the Ride

I entered college with the hopes of being an environmental engineer. Like so many in my age group, I caught the tail end of the environmental movement in the '70s—and then it started to fizzle. So I changed my major and got caught up in the business of making money, or to rephrase that, the business of *chasing* money.

In 1985, I began traveling extensively for work and had the opportunity to see the rest of the world. While working in Mexico, Korea, Taiwan, the United Kingdom, and Japan, I found that these countries, like the United States, were all confronting similar environmental challenges.

As time went on, I became more and more restless. At first I thought it was my job, so I changed jobs. That wasn't it. Then I thought it must be because I was a budding entrepreneur, so I started my own successful business.

But it wasn't any of those things, and I finally came to the conclusion that I was in the wrong field and that my original inclination to work with the environment had been correct. I also began to worry that the world was on some kind of collision course with the concept of "finite resources." Early evidence of this was the decline in the world's rainforests. Most important, I realized that we humans, with our technology and consumptive tendencies, were the culprits behind much of the damage to these natural systems.

In 1987, I told myself that I would once again get involved in the environmental arena. However, I was conflicted. I had become accustomed to a lifestyle that was not frivolous, but not exactly frugal, either. Now, I could afford what I needed when I needed it and some luxuries to boot.

I had also developed a good reputation, along with my successful business. I was not sure that I was willing to give all this up and make the transition to environmental zealot.

It was at this moment that I had an opportunity to link up with some of my old friends from earlier in my life, when I was pondering an environmental career. Fresh out of college, I had been involved in trekking and mountain climbing expeditions, and my friend, Lane Larson, and I climbed Mt. Orizaba in an effort to set a world record for the highest altitude scuba dive. This was a semi-active volcano with a pool of water at the summit above 18,000

The web of life in southern Ohio—an Eastern Box Turtle; a Whitetail Fawn in spring; and the very vocal American Bullfrog.

Sunrise on the farm.

feet. As I was contemplating this adventure with Lane and his wife, Wanda, he nudged me about our many talks about my becoming an environmental engineer.

And, as only a good friend can do, Lane also reminded me that my life in business was somewhat superficial and that if I didn't begin making changes soon, I would probably become very successful in business, but not a truly fulfilled human being. I decided to opt for change, and soon thereafter, the planning for the ride really began to take shape.

In 1988, I attended an "Up with People" performance at the Al-Marah Arabian horse ranch in Tucson. My friend, Tracy Church, and I were invited to this performance by her sister's husband, Dale, who was a vice-president in the organization.

The performance was held in an outdoor show ring. I was impressed with the facility, and asked Tracy and Dale to introduce me to the owners of the farm, but we couldn't find Mrs. Tankersley in time for an introduction. However, as we were leaving, Dale pointed her out in the crowd. Then, we took a drive around the property and I realized how enormous the operation truly was. We stopped by the main office to pick up some promotional material on the ranch and then left. But I continued thinking about Al-Marah days later, and I sensed there was a connection to explore at some future date.

The Al-Marah ranch was nestled down low along a small stream that came out of the mountains and, as a result, was hidden from view. More than 200 acres in size, it was located in the heart of a growing residential area on the east side of Tucson. Today, it is home to about 450 Arabian horses year round. The operation also includes ranches in two other Arizona locations.

At the time, I was a partner in two businesses. We had a manufacturing and assembly operation in Tucson and a much larger operation in Hermosillo, Sonora, Mexico. We assembled products for other companies, such as Laidlaw drip-dry coat hangers, IBM computer circuit boards, radios for the U.S. military, the Wonder Bra, and a host of other products.

I had received an invitation to attend the "Up with People" performance at the Al-Marah Arabian ranch at the right time, knowing from my research that any attempt at a cross-country ride would have to be well financed and well organized. To achieve that, I would need credibility and a track record. I needed winners, people who could go the distance and were committed to the event.

After returning from the ranch, I spoke with several people about Al-Marah and found the general consensus to be that if Mrs. Tankersley decided to take on a project, it was as good as done. I wanted to set up a meeting with her, so I put together a brief letter and sent it by Federal Express to get her attention. Four days later, I got a phone call from the Al-Marah marketing director at my office in Tucson setting up a meeting.

When I met with our potential benefactor, I explained my interest in the rainforest issue, and my belief that the ride could bring attention to this cause. I believed that people along the route and the public in general would not be familiar with the issue and its implications.

Therefore, a Ride Across America and the attraction people have for horses could help us break the ice and allow us to introduce the issue to the general public. I told Mrs. Tankersley how committed I was and that we could, in fact, make it across the country with good planning and strong support.

My final argument was that to do it right and gain publicity for the issue, I had to instill the belief in people that we could make it. To convince them, I needed some credibility because at that point, I didn't have any. I told her that her commitment and support would give the ride the credibility we needed to bring on two environmental groups and several other co-sponsors.

To my great delight, she actually said, "Yes." Now, we were off, if not at a full gallop, at a fast trot!

My next step was to sign up the two most appropriate environmental groups I could find. I needed strong anchors on both the east and west coasts and preferably in Washington, D.C., so I went after Rainforest Action Network (RAN) and the Environmental Policy Institute (EPI). My first call was to RAN, where I was put through to Randy Hayes, the Executive Director, who thought the idea of the cross-country ride had some potential. However, he was not entirely convinced that we could finish.

Randy loved the idea from a "grass roots" standpoint and thought that if we could complete the event, it would be an appealing story that could draw attention to the endangered rainforests. I offered to send him some material, again by FedEx, the next day.

On my next trip back East on business, I met with the people from the Environmental Policy Institute, as well as my Congressman, Jim Kolbe. The presentation to the Environmental Policy Institute went well, and CEO Michael Clark walked out with me afterward. He told me a ride across America was an impressive idea and that he would give it serious thought.

Several weeks later, the EPI had a meeting with its board of directors and the idea for the ride was on the agenda. Most of the board members were a little concerned about the lack of financing, the safety issue, and the odds of whether we could, in fact, make it. When EPI staff member Sharon Benjamin mentioned to the board that Mrs. Tankersley had agreed to support the ride, EPI board member Marie Ridder spoke up and stated, "If Bazy is involved, it's on the up-and-up." As a result, the vote to participate went through and I had my first environmental group.

Excited, I then called Randy Hayes at RAN, told him we had EPI's support, and asked him to participate as well. He agreed to come on board, and we had our two groups! Congressman Kolbe also agreed to support us, so all in all, it was a very productive trip to D.C.

On the shuttle back, I found out that all flights were delayed because Mikhail Gorbachev was returning from his tour of New York. As a result, there was a major traffic jam, which for some reason slowed air traffic as well. Amazing, I thought, the impact one person can have on a metropolitan area the size of New York. He had shut down the whole city! I asked myself, "How are we ever going to ride a horse through here?"

Bazy at the training barn with the Australian-born stallion Bremervale Andronicus in November, 2009.

The Rainforest Action Network's successful 1980s campaign against World Bank funding of economic development projects in South America and other rainforest regions of the world.

ABOVE Lucian would ride all night and into the early morning and then drive sometimes 100s of miles to speak with a group of supporters like this group in St. Louis, Missouri.

OPPOSITE March Along, Ted Danson, and Lucian saddling up for a ride after the press conference in Tucson, 1989.

When one becomes involved in an event like this, or any other major undertaking, one has to jump in with both feet to pull it off. However, this is often easier said than done.

Case in point: I'm Lucian Spataro, an entrepreneur and business owner known in Tucson for my expertise in manufacturing. Suddenly, I begin asking friends if I should take nine months off without pay so I can train and ride a horse across America. Predictably, many of my friends thought I was crazy.

My friends and peers at the time tended to be more concerned with the chit-chat at the local bar, Fridays, after work than about environmental concerns. As I look back now, all of us were chasing the money and each other. It was becoming clear to me as I looked around that time moves like smoke through a keyhole, and if you don't manage the wisp that it is, you'll wake up 20 years later with nothing to show for your efforts. With these pressing thoughts on my mind, the ride across America began to consume my every waking moment.

I decided to cut back to a half-day at our business and worked from noon till about 4:00 p.m. daily, spending the morning and then late into each evening training and working on the ride. Our training was simply to ride and ride and ride some more. The horses, as well as I, needed to get used to traffic and their new daily routine.

I rode each day at 4:00 a.m. or 5:00 a.m., as I would have to do on the ride, ending at around 11:00 a.m. We spent a lot of time on the streets of Tucson during early morning rush-hour traffic. Sometimes, I saw friends on their way to work at 7:00 a.m. Those encounters ran like this:

"Are you heading for work, Lucian?"

"Yeah, you need a ride?"

I began working on a regular basis on strategy and training with Dr. Cartwright and Dr. Hancock at Al-Marah. As you might guess, this schedule put a real damper on my social life and consequently, my girlfriend moved to San Francisco. Afterward, I threw myself even more actively into the training process.

In January 1989, we put together a press conference to kick off the event and started serious training. We invited environmentalist and actor Ted Danson, Randy Hayes and Michael Clark to Al-Marah. Ted Danson had recently started his own environmental organization, the American Oceans Campaign (AOC), and was familiar with EPI. In classic Danson style, he spoke as one who truly cared, and it was obvious to all that he understood the issues. The media picked up on this and the conference went off very well.

Mrs. Tankersley and Al-Marah rolled out the red carpet and walked March Along, the horse I'd be riding, into the room in which the press conference was being held. This really caught the media by surprise, and gave me my first class in Media Management 101. At this first press conference, I studied closely as Danson and the others controlled the exchange of information, constantly redefining and focusing what they said so that what would appear in the papers and on the news would be clear and on point. I knew I would have to learn this technique quickly if we were to be successful with the media aspect of this event.

"When Lucian first came to me with the proposal to use Arabian horses for a coast-to-coast ride to bring attention to our issue, I loved the gutsiness of the idea...a real grassroots approach. It worked wonderfully and became the event that you will read about today."

—Randy Hayes
Founder
Rainforest Action Network

OPPOSITE A big part of organizing and completing the ride was administrative and included fund-raising with very helpful donors like Mrs. William Randolph Hearst, applying for and obtaining 66 permits and or route approval from hundreds of municipalities and government entities, and then also the related insurance that was required to use the faster "along the string" route we rode.

After the interviews were over, we had a chance to do some riding. Ted Danson, Bob Sulnick, Randy Hayes and I all took off for a short ride around the ranch. From that point on, I was increasingly excited about the event as it began to gather momentum, and turned over operational control of the business in Tucson to my partners.

I was now working full time on the ride and on training for it. I set up a timetable for activities that we needed to complete and used this schedule to coordinate with both environmental groups. To firm up the route, I needed to negotiate with each state to use the road I wanted, and they would either require that I had a shadow vehicle, or no support vehicle.

In the western states of the ride, only the permit was required, and no support vehicle. In the east, states often required that we had a vehicle in high-traffic areas and that I avoid rush-hour traffic. To our surprise, some states allowed horse traffic to actually take precedence over vehicular traffic!

In most states, no permits were required on secondary roads, and in those states I rode on through. In the west, however, we were traveling the Interstate, which required dozens of permits, it seemed.

Our insurance policy was with Lloyds of London, and we worked with the Equestrian Department of Lloyds and the directing manager, Adrian Pratt, to obtain this policy. We also purchased horse mortality insurance and personal injury insurance: $250,000 for myself and the other team members .

On behalf of the ride, Al-Marah sent letters to clients and friends like Michael Landon and Mrs. William Randolph Hearst, who agreed to serve on the board of advisors for the ride. Soon thereafter, Mrs. Hearst sent a check to help in our fund-raising efforts.

Mrs. Tankersley had given me the number for the Hearst Castle in California, so I called to thank her for the financial support. I was completely unprepared when she answered the phone. We spoke for about 20 minutes, and after that phone call, I felt that we had a very good chance of finishing the ride and raising a substantial sum of money.

We still had a couple of other holes to fill. We needed a crew person to handle the horses, a vehicle to take the place of the English coach, and a shadow vehicle as well. We needed an alternative to steel shoes for the horses and we needed more corporate sponsorship. I also needed more help from both environmental groups. The Rainforest Action Network and I were doing most of the work, and EPI was just hanging in there with us as a sponsor in name only.

Although EPI had committed to help, they simply could not organize sufficiently in the midst of their pending merger with Friends of the Earth (FOE). Their lack of involvement led to several very emotional phone conversations. One thing led to another and EPI/FOE flew in an outside consultant named Bob Harvey to give them his opinion of our project. I spoke with Bob for over six hours. He gave me a copy of his six-page report on the status of the ride, and I agreed with almost everything he said. I thought the report was extremely accurate.

J. H. SILVERSMITH

May 1, 1989

Ride Across America
ATTENTION: Lucien Spataro
5620 North Kolb
Suite 173
Tuscon, AZ 85715

RE: Policy #: GLA303861

Dear Lucien:

Enclosed is the above caption
with an annual premium of $2,
$2,886.85 is enclosed which i
inspection fee. This policy

If you have any questions, pl

Yours truly,

Czech, ARM, CIC

STATE of INDIANA   INDIANAPOLIS

INDIANA DEPARTMENT OF HIGHWAYS   Room 1101, State Office Building
100 North Senate Avenue   317-232-5533
Indianapolis, Indiana 46204-2249

April 18, 1989

Lucian Spataro
RIDE ACROSS AMERICA
5620 North Kolb, Suite 173
Tucson, Arizona 85715

RE: Permit Information Concerning
RIDE ACROSS AMERICA Event

Dear Mr. Spataro:

This letter is in response to your request concerning a permit from the Indiana Department of Highways for the Ride Across America event.

The Indiana Department of Highways do not require a permit for an individual to ride a horse on U.S. 50 right-of-way. We do request you honor the following requirements.

1. Your letter states this event is insured by Lloyds of London, please send a copy of the certificate to the Indiana Department of Highways: 100 North Senate Avenue, Indianapolis, Indiana 46204-2249. Attention: Robert D. Cales, Room 1108.

...ler are not to interfere with the motoring public
...ved surface except as necessary to cross inter-
... etc.

...re to manage such that they do not interfere nor
... flow of traffic.

... the Indiana State Police (317/232-8248) of your
... approximate time schedule for your travels in the
...

...ses all of your concerns. Good luck with your event,
...ture help, please don't hesitate to telephone my

Sincerely yours,

Robert D. Cales
Permit Services Engineer

RDC/sl

An Equal Opportunity Employer

WILLIAM RANDOLPH HEARST, JR.
959 8TH AVENUE
NEW YORK, NY 10019

3709

PAY TO THE
ORDER OF___Ride Across America___   Jan. 3, 1989   1-30/210

Two-thousand Five-hundred and 00/100-------- $ 2,500.00

MANUFACTURERS
HANOVER
MANUFACTURERS HANOVER TRUST COMPANY
959 EIGHTH AVENUE
NEW YORK, N.Y. 10019   ATTORNEY
                                              ----------DOLLARS
FOR Contribution)

⑆021000306⑆ 101406550326 5⑆ 3709

INSURANCE AGENTS - BROKERS   825 EAST SPEER BLVD. DENVER

As a result, I was shocked when EPI/FOE chose to withdraw from the event six months after they initially agreed to be part of it and one month before the start of the ride! While at the time, their withdrawal seemed catastrophic, looking back it was a blessing in disguise. It allowed us to regroup and to focus and rally a smaller and more active team, which in turn helped us get organized.

From that point on, we moved at a much quicker pace. Two of the board members, Leslie Barclay and Marie Ridder, who represented EPI on the "Ride Across America" board stayed on with us, which helped lessen the impact of EPI's official withdrawal. These people, along with the rest of the board members, became very important to us during the event.

One of our big concerns was funding. With two months left to go, we barely had enough funds to complete the event. Fortunately, The Rainforest Action Network was confident enough and committed enough to carry us for the balance. Randy Hayes was utterly committed to the ride, which bolstered our morale. The railroad companies fell through and so did JB Spirits.

Later, Chevron came through with an educational grant to RAN on behalf of RAN's educational efforts, one of which that summer was the ride. By May, we had enough funding to get the ride off the ground and hoped that further efforts along the way would raise the balance.

We were still having some problems determining which saddle we were going to use, and were struggling with when we might need to switch to Easyboots to preserve the horses' feet. I also assembled a list of farriers who might help us care for the horses' feet while we were crossing the country.

The strategy we settled on was to ride using the steel shoes as far as we could go. Then, we'd switch to Easyboots for the balance of the ride.

The choice of a saddle and riding gear was not as easy, and took some experimentation. We started the ride with the EPIC Endurance saddle, endurance stirrups, a cantle bag, a pommel bag, a saddle pad and a saddle blanket, a water bottle, lead rope, stethoscope, a watch and flashlight. As the ride wore on, I began to jettison much of this equipment and changed saddle and blanket combinations in search of the best combination. Through trial and error we eventually ended up with a single wool blanket, a Porter endurance saddle, a water bottle and collapsible water bucket, a cantle bag and a pommel bag. The larger and heavier Porter saddle was much better at distributing my weight over the horse's back.

I kept the endurance stirrups when I made a saddle switch. These stirrups were instrumental in allowing me to ride the distances I did each day. They were much wider than a normal stirrup and averaged about 3" front to rear. They were also padded and much more comfortable and practical than narrow stirrups. Much of the gear we eventually settled on was supplied to us by Patty Phelan as a donation from her company's catalog.

Many people asked me how I chose the route. My first concern was time and weather, and my second concern was media exposure. I wanted the shortest path possible that would present us with the greatest opportunity to talk with people about this issue.

Easyboot PATENTED ®

ABOVE Switching to Easyboots in Arizona was a critical decision point in the ride. These boots protect the hoof and allowed us to ride through rough terrain and often areas that had broken glass on the side of the road, additionally, they were not slippery on asphalt.

OPPOSITE Promoting the ride, and in turn the rainforest issue, was a big part of the event and publications and sponsors like the Phelan catalog were a big help in getting the word out.

Suzan Victoria

Lucian Spataro and AM March Along training for a real "cross country" ride.

...hooling

...er who wants one
...y-crafted leather
...which different
...and reins can be
...igh-grade
...erials and
...—fine full grain
...10 stitches to
...ead of the usual
...and-finished.
...headstall is
...le from both
...roat latch and
...nd (shown, but
...with a raised
...and). To order
...her products,
...ead size and
...ark chestnut

...Headstall

...Noseband

RIDE ACROSS AMERICA

...band

...orn a few
...nostrils in
...hin groove
...o a horse
...bit.

...dropped
...the
...ightly
...asically a
...eband
...ps that
...iece.
...8 $44

Figure Eight Noseband
The top rear strap of the figure eight noseband exerts gentle pressure on the horse's cheeks while the lower straps are like the dropped noseband. Perfect for cross country.
■ *Figure Eight #209* **$44**

Headstall Reins
To complete the matched headstall set, choose from the styles below:
■ *Plain 5/8 inch Flat Rein #223* **$44**
■ *Laced 5/8 inch Rein #224* **$55**
■ *Rubber Grip (Leather-Backed) Rein, #225* **$60**

EPIC General Purpose Saddle
A beautifully designed saddle for the versatile rider —anyone whose weekly routine may include flatwork, schooling fences, trail riding, you name it. Unlike a forward-seat saddle, this General Purpose saddle has a deep seat and a long straight flap. Minimal knee rolls provide added support. We've added two D-rings on each side of the saddle for trail riding (although not pictured in photo). The General Purpose differs from our EPIC Endurance Saddle in its narrower waist, narrower seat, and lighter weight (only 13 pounds), but has EPIC's customary impeccable British quality. Medium and wide tree widths, seat sizes 16, 17, and 18-inch, in black or dark chestnut brown.
■ *General Purpose #116* **$925**
When ordering your saddle please inquire about our full line of saddle accessories.

EPIC Endurance Saddle

The EPIC Endurance Saddle
What's most conspicuous about this international-award-winning saddle is the high quality of British craftsmanship, but what's most important about it is the extraordinary comfort it provides for both horse and rider. It was designed for competitive endurance riders, but it will reward anyone who spends much time in the saddle.

From the horse's perspective: the spring tree has panels which extend beyond the cantle, maximizing the distribution of the rider's weight. The saddle's cut-back head prevents impact on the withers, and a deeper than usual gullet increases airflow along the horse's spinal column, reducing overheating and fatigue.

Don't you sometimes want to get on your horse and just keep going? You can ride anywhere. Beginning in May 1989, Lucian Spataro and his Arab gelding, AM March Along, are riding across America–in this case to help draw support for global environmental causes. Some of Phelan's staffers are riding a few miles with him. Perhaps you'd like to join him if he rides through your neighborhood. The planned route goes from Los Angeles to New York City with stops in Flagstaff, Albuquerque, Amarillo, Oklahoma City, St. Louis, Indianapolis, Columbus, Pittsburgh, Harrisburg, and Philadelphia. Individuals or companies that would like to donate funds (for each mile completed) may do so with the proceeds going to Rainforest Action Network and The Environmental Policy Insitute. For more information call EPI at 202-544-2600.

EPIC Multi-Bridle

EPIC Multi-Bridle
The most convenient, versatile, and sporty-looking leather bridle around, made in England by EPIC of fine black leather and solid brass fittings. Great for trail riding—you can securely tie your horse and drop the bit for feeding or watering. There are six brass buckles for easy adjustment, assuring correct fit and access from either side of the horse. The flat leather is the most popular, but for a dressier look the rolled leather beautifully sets off a fine head. Both styles available in full or cob size in either black or dark brown leather.
■ *Multi-Bridle with Flat Leather #210* **$94**
■ *Matching Flat Reins #211* **$48**
■ *Multi-Bridle with Rounded Leather #215* **$140**
■ *Matching Rounded Reins #216* **$56**

From the rider's perspective: the saddle is built with a deep, comfortable seat. The extended flaps allow the rider to remain long in the leg with close horse contact, staying balanced and upright even when traveling over rough ground. The black leather saddle weighs 14 pounds, in medium and wide width, in sizes 16, 17, and 18-inch. Also available in dark chestnut brown leather by special order.
■ *EPIC Saddle #101* **$975**

When ordering your saddle please inquire about our full line of saddle accessories.

F or telephone orders call 415-332-6001

I took out a map of the United States and a string, and located the two largest cities, Los Angeles and New York. Then I laid the string down on the map in a straight line from L.A. to New York. I then taped the string to the map and stuck it on the wall. That was going to be my route, or as close to it as possible. The shortest path between two points is a straight line, so I concluded that the closer I could stay to this line, the shorter the timeframe for the ride.

Further calculations showed that the straight route, as the crow flies along the string, was about 2,200 miles, using the legend on the map. I knew I could not ride right along the string because in many places there were no roads. We needed water and feed, and we needed to make good time.

I knew from experience that it was much faster riding along a road than bushwhacking across the desert or some other wilderness area. With this in mind, using local and regional topographical and street maps, I then found all of the roads, highways, and trails that were parallel with this string. Staying as close to the string as I could, I simply highlighted these routes, connecting super highways with power lines and then secondary roads and so on until I had my own route along that string.

In the end, the route ended up being a mish-mash of roads, highways, power lines, railroad rights-of-way and ad-libbing. This route meandered north and south of the string, adding about 800 miles to the route, but generally we tried to stay as close to that string as we possibly could.

I then calculated the distance and our pace, located the various metropolitan areas along the route, and began working with Francesca Vietor at RAN to schedule media events and fund-raisers. I obtained the permits in the same manner, systematically working with each state along the master route until we had three folders full of permits and letters of approval for specific routes.

This ride was both an endurance ride and a media event. These two goals were not always compatible with each other, which made the actual riding and the planning for this event difficult. Often we were torn between riding farther on a particular day and altering our route so we could make a media commitment. Our need to meet both our media commitments and our ride goals was an ongoing cause for debate and discussion among team members and others involved.

On the one hand, I would suggest to anyone inclined to try to break our record that they focus on the ride and not use it to attract attention to a specific issue. Even though that focus was successful in accomplishing our objective, it could sap your energy and slow you down.

On the other hand, I thought when I first began the ride that our team could make the crossing in four months. I now believe that a team in that timeframe using three horses and one rider would need to rest a week for every month of riding, which we essentially ended up doing. Looking back, I believe our short rests along the way were essential and that the media commitments helped break the routine. This led to a much-needed injection of energy and enthusiasm.

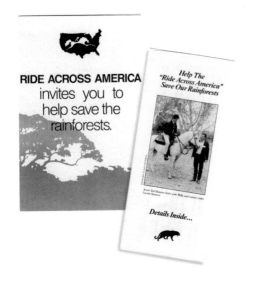

The ride was both an endurance ride and a media event. These brochures doubled as both an information packet and mailer for those we met along the way who were inclined to donate money to our cause.

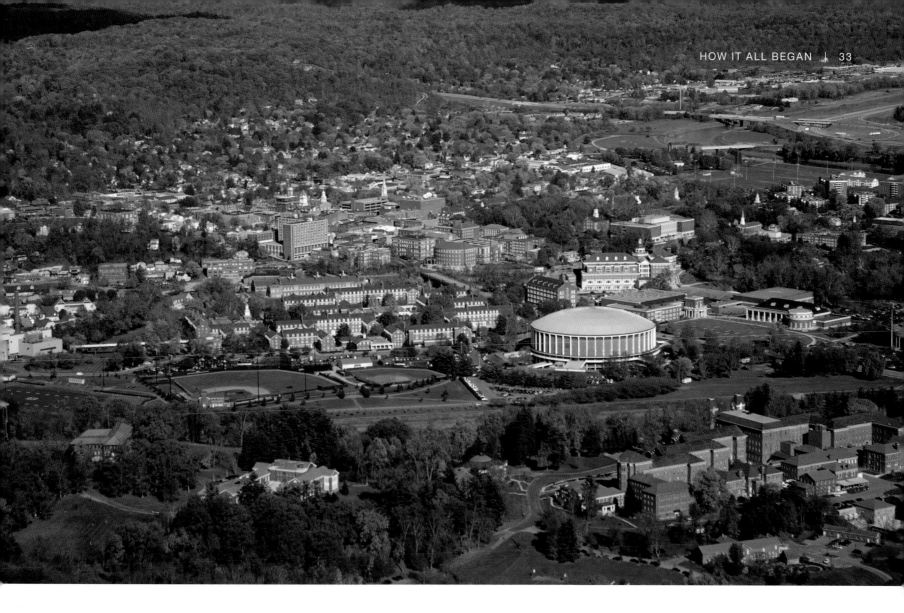

The training, when combined with the ride itself, would be nearly a year-long, very strenuous event, and for me its purpose—to bring attention to the rainforest issue—was a significant motivator. If it were not for this objective, and for the many people we met along the way who were now cheering us on, we might not have reached our goal.

On a side note, when I first started thinking about getting back into the environmental arena, I considered finishing my Master's in Environmental Studies as a good first step. I settled on Ohio University and their environmental program within the Geology Department. Geoff Smith, the head of that program, and I spoke on several occasions, and after the ride, in 1990, I decided to take the leap and enrolled in the program. I ultimately completed a Ph.D.

This is the abbreviated version of the planning and significant events behind the ride. There are many more activities that took place and countless other details that we had to contend with, but those described above were the most significant.

Athens, home to Ohio University, is a historic college town located along the scenic Hocking River in southeastern Ohio. Athens is a real "tree hugger" community and a qualified Tree City as recognized by the National Arbor Day Foundation and a beautiful city in the fall of the year.

LOS ANGELES

CHAPTER TWO:
LIFE ALONG THE SANTA ANA RIVER

It was 6:00 a.m. on May 19, 1989, as the dawn began lighting the Pacific surf. AM Sweet William (Willy) and I waded into the surf on California's Huntington Beach and then rode up onto the sand heading east on the first leg of our long journey. The Santa Ana River in years past would empty into the Pacific at this point. However, it no longer flowed, so we decided to use the river bed as our route through Los Angeles.

Our goal was to begin knee-deep in saltwater on the West Coast and finish four to six months later knee-deep in saltwater on the East Coast. By doing so, we could draw attention to the various environmental problems worldwide, especially the depletion of the rainforests. What better way to draw attention to the whole messy affair than to ride a horse across America?

ABOVE, BELOW and OPPOSITE Lucian and Willy, May 19, 1989, just as the sun was coming up on the beach in California, 2,963 miles yet to go.

Mojave Desert

LOS ANGELES

SAN BERNADINO

Lake Havasu

HUNTINGTON BEACH

Salton Sea

ABOVE The route through California was a test of extremes with 50 degree temperatures on the coast and millions of people to 130 degrees temperatures in the desert and a landscape void of human life as far as the eye can see.

OPPOSITE Willy and Lucian standing on an LA street corner in the asphalt jungle perusing the map and wondering, "How in the heck are we ever going to time this light and clear this many lanes of traffic".

I was sitting on my white horse at a street corner in Los Angeles on the first leg of my coast-to-coast ride across America, and I could see Anaheim Stadium off to my left. My horse and I were waiting to cross eight lanes of rush-hour traffic, listening to horns honking and brakes screeching.

My eyes were already stinging from the gas fumes, smog, and exhaust, and it was almost 100 degrees and getting hotter. I had chosen to wear running tights, Nike 990 running shoes, a baseball cap and a small backpack. Hanging off each side of Willy's saddle were two of my shirts, resting beside a water canteen and lead rope.

Standing on my left, on the street corner, was a man and his shopping cart full of clothes, cans and bottles. On my right was a young lady with a set of headphones on and a bright yellow running outfit, jogging in place. Behind me was an older man in a business suit, complete with a tie and a briefcase.

We were all waiting for the light to change. I had arrived at the corner first, so I was closest to the street. I let the reins drop a bit and begin to peruse my L.A. street map. I was really in no hurry—after all, I still had 3,000 miles to go.

The sight of Willy and me standing on a street corner reading our L.A. street map, waiting for the light to change, must have been startling for the commuters this Friday morning. I had already noticed that when the light changed, or just prior, people already had one foot on the gas and one foot on the brake. The second thing that caught my attention was that you never had enough time to cross eight lanes of traffic before the light changed to green in favor of the drivers. They looked neither left nor right to clear the pedestrian lane, but assumed it was clear. After all, what idiot would take that long to cross eight lanes of traffic?

While my three fellow street-crossers made it to the other side in a flash, it took me a second longer to get moving, and that second cost me. As soon as L.A. drivers saw the crossing light turn orange, they released their brakes in anticipation of the green light. The problem with being on a horse was that I invariably got caught in the fourth or fifth lane as I tried to cross, and quickly found myself surrounded by traffic. I tried trotting across, but Willy, with steel horseshoes on, had a slippery time of it. A slower approach was much better, especially with all the noise and commotion. A horse moving quickly across asphalt can easily get out of control. Welcome to "The Ride Across America!"

Throughout this event—and specifically in L.A.—the natural obstacles of sun, rain, wind, and often topography presented fewer problems than did the man-made obstacles we encountered. These included highways, cattle-guards, fences, homes, streetlights, bridges, and cars and trucks by the millions. They were a constant source of danger and would inevitably force us to reroute, or schedule night rides, to avoid them.

In 1989, crossing America in anything other than a car required permits, permits, and more permits. These were for beaches, roads, highways, parks, streets, towns, cities, and counties—you name it. If you went through any of these on a horse, a permit was required.

The gas fumes, smog, and exhaust were overwhelming and it was getting hotter by the minute as we rode through the streets of L.A.

It took us over two years in advance of the ride to define the route and obtain all the permits the route required! Of those 67-plus permits, California required over 30 percent, or 21 permits in total.

Apparently, there wasn't much you could do in California without a permit: to get onto the beach, be on the beach, or ride off the beach required that we obtain six permits from four different governmental groups. Fortunately, when people learned that our cause was saving the rainforests, it helped us break the ice with various government agencies and get some of the permits faster than usual.

To get from the beach to just west of Los Angeles was in itself very difficult. The area was crisscrossed with numerous super-highways, fences, and a mish-mash of residential areas and roads. Our first day of riding was in the dry Santa Ana river bed and along its banks.

That first day, riding in the river bed and skirting around it required that we often went up into the dreaded rush hour traffic. On four occasions, we were forced to cross eight lanes of traffic that was zipping by at a speed of 40–60 m.p.h.

On one occasion, Willy and I were riding down a small residential street in an effort to bypass a bridge crossing. The sidewalk was very narrow and we were riding downhill. The road meandered in long curves through the neighborhood, and on my right was a neck-high brick wall. As I rode into one of these long curves, we came up parallel to a yard with a huge Doberman and a smaller yapping terrier. I could see both dogs from my seat in the saddle. This wasn't a problem because Willy could sense they were on the other side of the fence and not dangerous. Nevertheless, he was still shying toward the road to our left.

At that very moment, a city bus pulled up on our left at a bus stop that we were approaching. Just as people were beginning to disembark, I noticed that we had walked into a box canyon of sorts. There was the bus to my left, barking dogs to my right, and twenty people straight ahead, all gawking and pointing at us.

I could have simply stopped and waited for the group to break up, and then rode on through, and those were my intentions. But when I was about ten feet from the disembarking passengers, I halted when I heard a terrifying noise. Coming up from behind on the long curve, blind to this very complicated box canyon of people, buses, horses and dogs, was someone on a skateboard. The rhythm of the wheels on the board, broken every few seconds by a seam in the sidewalk, was unnerving, but we had no place to go and I could tell that the board was picking up speed.

Willy heard it, too, but the danger didn't register with the people in front of me. They were either accustomed to skateboards or they didn't hear this one over the barking dogs and the traffic. I couldn't move right toward the fence with the barking dogs, and the bus was still a minute or two from pulling away on my left. My only chance was either to move forward, or to hold our ground and hope that the board rider, when he came around the corner, could recover within about 15 feet, adjust, or stop.

To settle Willy down, I reined him around so he could see what was coming at him. This helped, but the closer the board came to that corner, the more Willy backed toward the people who were now behind us and not dispersing, even though I told them to walk away quickly. I had to keep Willy on the sidewalk because in the grass on both sides of the sidewalk were sprinkler heads. They were sticking up and could do real damage to Willy's feet, not to mention the surprise of knocking one of those off and spraying water up into the air. We found ourselves confined to the slippery sidewalk with the skateboard on its way toward us.

The skateboard came around the corner and the girl on it was going even faster than I had expected. Her first reaction was surprise, then panic. Rather than hit us, she jumped off the board and let it go right through Willy's legs (we were standing at a slight angle—no special planning on my part) and then into the crowd.

A boy in the crowd caught the board and gave it back to the girl, who was now talking with me. This all happened so fast that, before Willy could respond in terror, the board was already through his legs and heading into the crowd. The whole incident took less than a minute, but I learned a very important lesson from that brief encounter: expect the unexpected!

It came in handy later in West Virginia while climbing Cheat Mountain and its 52 switchbacks. I knew that, whenever possible, we should ride on the side of the road that gave us the most room on both sides, and gave us the longest view ahead and behind us. This applied even in a slow residential area.

On several occasions as we rode along the river, we met homeless people who lived in the river bed under the bridges, as well as in cardboard boxes, old cars and drainage culverts. As we rode down one trail that skirted the river, the trail often meandered down into the river bed to avoid fences that came up against the river.

In those cases, Willy and I rode down into the sandy bottom of the river and later came back up onto the edge. Riding along the river bed, I came upon a small group of holes dug into the embankment. It looked as if some neighborhood children had been playing war games and, in the process, had dug bunkers in the embankment in which to hide.

The embankment was sharply steep and rose up about 30 feet to the top of the river bed. There were numerous trails coming from the top of the embankment to the entrance of these holes. There was also quite a bit of debris at the entrance of each hole. It didn't really dawn on me until I saw a shopping cart at the head of one of these trails that people were actually living in these earth caves.

On another occasion in the dry river bed, I saw that the pylons supporting the bridge and anchored in the dry river bed acted as a fourth wall in a three-sided cardboard house or a box. I rode through one of these encampments just as some of the homeless were waking up. There were some coals from small cooking fires still burning from the night before, and people were gathered around these fires or at the entrance of the box houses. Our trail went right up into one encampment, but no one said a word as we rode through.

Willy was not an enthusiastic participant in these encounters and I sensed that he could feel the misery around us. It was a very uncomfortable contrast to ride into eight lanes of L.A. traffic with BMWs, Mercedes, earphones and convenience stores on every corner right after having ridden through an encampment of homeless people. I doubt that many people driving on those bridges knew about those who lived under them and in the river bed.

Earlier that morning, just as the sun was beginning to rise and we were coming up out of the dry river bed, we had ridden past several employees walking to work at a power plant. They stopped short as I rode up, and I said, "Hello!"

They just stared, and then, before they turned to go into the plant, one yelled out, "Where are you riding from?"

I answered, "The beach."

I quickly came to expect the inevitable next question: "Where are you going?"

I remember my response as though it were yesterday and we were in slow motion. I reined Willy around to face them, looked each one in the eye, and said with as straight a face as I could muster, "New York." I'll never forget the look on their faces.

Just as they were going to ask another question, the whistle blew and they all ran inside. As they were running in, I heard one person remark, "I think he's serious."

As I rode away, I thought to myself, "What an appropriate start!" It was at that moment that the significance of this ride really sank in. I realized that we were undertaking a very difficult task with 3,000 miles yet to go. Then, after the initial shock wore off, I remember smiling to myself, patting Willy on the neck, and saying out loud, "All the way! Let's do it, just me and you." This would be the first of many conversations I would have with Willy. I had a very strong, confident feeling that we were going to make it.

That pat on the neck reinforced the secret pact that Willy and I had made earlier. It was a very warm feeling on a very chilly morning, but as I look back now, it was naive of me to believe that this was going to be an easy trip. Our pact was actually going to be hard to fulfill—I had no clue about the hurdles yet to come!

About six miles from the beach, a golf course bordered the river and I could find no alternate route. Our tracks left large divots in the fairway as we cantered across to the ringing words, "BALLLLLLL." Several golfers were teeing up for an early morning foursome. Much to their surprise, the course that morning presented a new and different hazard—a white Arabian horse and rider cantering along the fairway toward the river.

It was a very hot day and our only source of water was from the many convenience stores along the route. Each time I rode up, I was gratified to find a kindly person filling up with gas who was willing to hold Willy while I found us some water.

Three local riders, Allen Coward, Bob Smith, and Joe Wheatley, were scheduled to meet us about 12 miles up the river from the beach. Their job would be to help us traverse the complicated route from the beach up into Riverside County, the point of our first fund-raiser

at the Reinhold Arabian ranch. I had talked to Allen on the phone several days earlier and he'd told me he had identified a route.

We agreed to meet along the river. Although I didn't know what he looked like, I wasn't worried about finding him. I thought it unlikely that any other horseback riders would be riding there, and the river route was pretty straightforward. I was wrong.

The river bed was very wide in some places—as much as two or three football field lengths. I was riding on the west side and often had to leave the river to go over or around residential areas, bridges, and other human obstacles. After about five hours of riding I was sure we had ridden over 12 miles—but by my map, it was closer to 15! Now, I was getting a bit concerned that we had missed each other, but I kept on going.

Joe Wheatley, Allen Coward, and Bob Smith knew the horse trails in this area and they led us from the concrete jungle up into the mountains of Riverside County.

Finally, after Willy and I had gone about 16 miles up the river bed, we ran into Allen, Bob and Joe. They had been riding up and down the *other* side of the river bed, asking anyone they met if they'd seen us. Then they split up, and Joe ended up on my side of the river bed, eventually catching up with us from behind. We then found Bob and Allen and headed up off the river into some trails that only Allen knew.

Allen Coward, L.A.'s version of "The Man from Snowy River," helped us navigate over, around, and through the myriad man-made and natural obstacles that confronted us those first two days. I quickly realized that local riders like Allen would be our best sources of information, direction and guidance.

L.A. had been one heck of an initiation. No practice on the Tucson streets could have prepared us for what we encountered there. Later along the ride, we would often encounter the same obstacles to a greater or lesser degree.

We did have one satisfaction: for one ten-mile stretch, we found ourselves traveling faster than the cars we were riding alongside!

Allen, my new companion, was actually a local endurance rider and a blacksmith by choice. He spent every minute in the saddle when he wasn't working. I can honestly say that his support made getting through the concrete jungle both possible and safe.

Bob Smith was a friend of Allen's, and the two had teamed up to ride the Pacific Crest Trail from Mexico to Canada. Joe Wheatley was a retired Navy pilot from Orange County, California, who rode with us off and on from L.A. to the Colorado River, keeping me company for the next two weeks. We spent a lot of time together out of the saddle as well, scouting trails and locating camping spots.

It was 5:30 p.m. and Allen, Joe, Bob, and I had just met Bob's wife and my teammate, Sheryl Studley, a horse masseuse, about 29 miles from the ocean. Our meeting spot was at a secluded canyon on one of the last old ranches in Riverside, California. Rancho de la Sierra Vista sits on top of a saddle that overlooks Riverside County and the area we had just ridden through, just above Prado Dam.

Now, up in the mountains, we found the view from there spectacular! High above the cement city, we could see clear skies, mountain vistas and greenery everywhere and unlike down in the city, we could hear the hum of nature in the quiet night. What a contrast! Our campsite seemed a million miles away from the street corner near Anaheim stadium, gas and exhaust fumes, the homeless shelters all along the river, and the white sandy beach.

Willy was standing quietly, appearing to look over the view just as I was, a piece of hay hanging from his mouth. I thought, "He's probably wondering what the heck we rode through today, and why." That would not be the last time I caught Willy pondering our fate.

It had been a long day, and we had to get up at 4:00 a.m. to begin our 23-mile ride to the Reinhold Arabian ranch the next day. I fell asleep, exhausted, at 8:30 p.m. and blissfully slept straight through.

OPPOSITE *(from left to right)* The L.A. team – Ringo, Casper, Allen Coward, Melanie Coward, Joe Wheatley, Sunshine, Bob Smith, and Cinder.

CALIFORNIA

CHAPTER THREE:
THE HIGH DESERT AND DEATH VALLEY

ABOVE and BELOW Riding from the beach in L.A. up into the barren but beautiful Morongo Valley was first and foremost daunting. Morongo Valley lies along the western edge of the Mojave Desert and as such is generally dry; here we got our first taste of what it feels like to be really thirsty.

OPPOSITE There was no training that we could do that could have ever prepared us for winds like these. Like an unrelenting bumble bee throbbing deep in your ear canal all day long. Our route took us through San Gorgonian Pass and the Windmill Farms in California.

After we left Riverside, we rode through San Jacinto Valley along the Ramona Expressway and then up through Lamb Canyon and into the town of Beaumont. Riding along the north side of United States Interstate 10, we rode through San Gorgonio and Cabazon and then along a power and pipeline road through the Morongo Indian reservation. This route would eventually carry us up into the Windmill Farms and then farther north along State Highway 62 into Morongo Valley.

For the next three days, we rode east in forty and fifty-knot winds toward the local Windmill Farms and State Highway 62. It wasn't fun—those winds were unrelenting and, to take advantage of them, the area supported the largest windmill farm in the United States. The locals often said, "This is nothing. Sometimes the wind blows so hard we have to change zip codes."

The windmill farms were amazing to behold when we first saw them stretching across the valley, like a wave of white picket fences rolling from ridge to ridge. When I was about a day's ride away, they looked like small, high-tech sentinels out of a Star Wars film. Compared to the San Jacinto and San Gorgonio Mountains, the size of the windmills was hard to grasp. From a distance, I could never have envisioned the impact they would have on the horses and the challenge they would present as we attempted to maneuver our way through this area.

The next day's ride began about 5:00 a.m., three hours (10 miles) from the first ridge of windmills. The wind was down enough that I could wear my cap with the bill facing forward to keep out the sun. As the wind began to pick up in the late morning, I learned to turn the bill around or lose the cap. I don't learn easily and three days into this stretch I found myself on my third cap. Two lost caps were enough: I was bound and determined to keep this last one all the way through the Windmill Farms area.

The closer we came to the windmills, the more impressed I became with the increasing intensity of the wind on each successive ridge. I began to hear a faint buzz, which I first shrugged off as just the whistling wind, but the closer we got, the more intense it became until I felt my eardrums throbbing. The reverberation was rhythmic and it certainly shook up Willy when we approached a particular windmill whose rotor was moving slowly. The windmill would periodically cast a menacing shadow across our trail.

I didn't see Willy look up once. I myself couldn't if I'd wanted to— the wind was so intense that I couldn't keep my eyes open. Fine grains of sand were swirling everywhere, and both Joe and I struggled to keep the horses moving forward. Both horses kept trying to angle down the ridge and I yelled at Joe that we needed to get off the ridge and angle off to the left. He could not hear me, although he was only about 20 feet in front of me.

Compared to us, the windmills were immense. The base of each windmill was actually a small house, and each rotor was as long as three flagpoles. They appeared to be about the height of a water tower; from base to base, side by side, they were half the length of a football field. The windmills were slightly staggered, not directly side by side. I thought to myself, "What amazing energy!"

Windmills used to be as common as the rural mailbox in the early part of this century. But over the next few decades, electricity, oil, and gas slowly took over the energy market. Some people say that the windmill farms create visual pollution. But wind is a natural source of energy and by far a better environmental source than coal. Burning fossil fuels releases large amounts of carbon dioxide into the atmosphere. These blanket the earth, and the accumulation will not allow heat reflected off the earth's surface to escape into the atmosphere. This build-up over time creates a general warming of the earth's surface.

When we finally left the Windmill Farms area, we bushwhacked our way up into the high desert and a town called Morongo Valley. Sheryl Studley and her dog, Patches, were the other half of our team at this stage. Sheryl, a lawyer and an endurance enthusiast, had been

OPPOSITE The Joshua tree became an omen for our ride through this area. The Joshua tree was named by Mormon settlers who crossed the Mojave Desert in the mid-nineteenth century, saw the tree and thought its shape reminded them of a story in the Bible in which Joshua raises his hands to the sky in prayer for water.

ABOVE Larry Hobbs at his ranch in Twenty Nine Palms.
This was one hot stretch, south of Death Valley and
almost 300 feet below sea level. The team consumed
hundreds of gallons of water daily.

OPPOSITE Larry Hobbs and his horse Bob rode every
day on his ranch in the desert.

recruited by the Al-Marah Arabian Horse Ranch—Willy's home and the major sponsor of the ride. She would assist in every aspect of the horse-related portion of the event. Sheryl's job was to help coordinate water stops, scout campsites, and locate trails and routes—all highly important for the success of the trip.

You would think that when riding a horse across America you could simply stop at the end of each day's ride and make camp. Not so. In the West, water and feed and your proximity to them are very important. In many places, it is illegal to pull off onto the side of the road and set up a camp, so often we had to identify a base camp and ferry the team back and forth at the beginning and end of each day.

For example, we had a four-day base camp at a ranch east of Twenty-Nine Palms. It belonged to Larry Hobbs, a retired rodeo cowboy who let us stay free of charge. The first day we camped there, we rode out of Joshua Tree through Twenty-Nine Palms and right into camp at Larry Hobbs' ranch, about a 27-mile ride.

The next day, we rode out of camp and about 20 miles east of Larry's ranch to a region just south of Death Valley. There were no gas stations, stores, water, or any of the other necessities we needed to sustain the team, so at the end of each day we marked a spot on the side of the road with a pile of rocks or a big orange marker. Then, Sheryl would pick Willy and me up by trailer and take us back to Larry's ranch. The next morning, we would load Willy up and drive out into the desert. We found our marker from the afternoon before and began riding from that point on.

On the fourth morning, we loaded up the whole team and drove to the drop-off point. Sheryl left Willy and me and then drove east 60 or 80 miles to a predetermined base camp, where she set up camp. At noon she was back to pick up Willy and me. We were covering about 20 miles per day at that point, so in this case we would be about 40 miles west of camp.

We would ride 40, 60 or even 80 miles to each base camp, taking the trailer back and forth each evening and morning and then, repeating the same distance past each base camp.

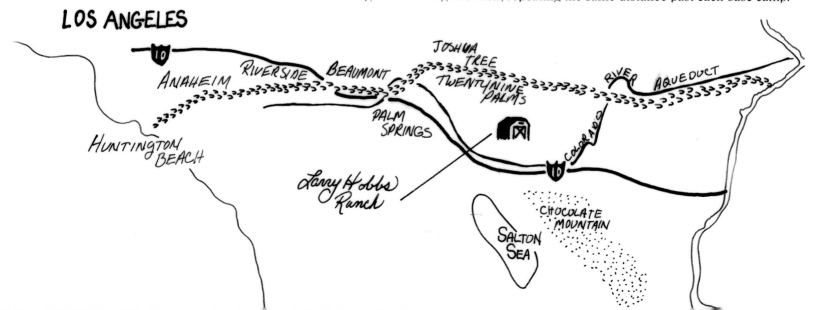

Then, we'd jump to the next base camp. In this manner we leapfrogged our way across the desert.

These were logistics I had planned for in Tucson (where I had been living before the ride), but I never actually had a chance to work through them until we got on the road. In planning the event, I knew that logistics and our route would play a very important role, so I spent hours poring over our route and alternate routes.

But because there were many items for which I could not plan, Sheryl and I spent the first two weeks working the bugs out of this system, trying to make it as efficient and safe as possible. Taking down the heavy corrals each morning and loading them onto the trailer at first took about twenty minutes. By the time we got to Larry's ranch, we had a system that took less than five minutes. We were pleased to see that some things were actually falling into place!

Sheryl and I were living in very cramped living quarters and had only known each other for under three weeks. It was what you could call a "trial marriage" of sorts. This was as much a people event as it was a horse or endurance event, so we initially spent a lot of time laying down the rules and creating personal do's and don'ts.

This planning and talking were very important because we were living together, whether we were basically compatible or not. The fact that we were very busy trying to establish a routine and a rhythm for an event that was so physically demanding was actually helpful. We had no time or energy to think much about any differences of opinion. Our focus was very short-term—the next 10 miles, the next water stop, the next campsite. This focus got us through the first couple of weeks: I call it our "honeymoon stage."

During those first three weeks, we spoke with the folks at Al-Marah daily about the horses and our route. The preparations back in Tucson had been, in some ways, very appropriate and in other ways, not terribly useful. The time I'd spent in Tucson training in traffic had been very helpful in California, but once I left Riverside, my traffic training was not used much. I actually didn't see a major city until Albuquerque, some 700 miles or five weeks later.

On the plus side, by the time we hit Albuquerque, New Mexico, a string of semis passing us within two feet didn't make Willy as much as lift an eyebrow. In fact, often on the highway or smaller two-lane roads, the rhythm of the cars swooshing by had a hypnotic effect on both Willy and me.

We tackled one problem after another and solved most, but one problem continued to baffle us. Willy was going through his first set of shoes faster than we had envisioned. Fifteen days into the ride, he needed new shoes. We knew this could be a major hurdle and that we needed to overcome it, or risk the success of the trip.

A horse's hooves grow slowly and a new set of shoes will usually last two months or longer, depending to a great extent on miles traveled. To secure a set of shoes to the hoof, you drive nails into the hoof wall. Typically, the hooves will grow out, and when you pull off the old shoes to reset or change them, the new hoof wall will be sufficient to find room for new nail holes.

ABOVE Loading and unloading the corrals each day, was a fast learning curve. Fifteen days into the event, our initial twenty minute exercise would take us only five minutes.

OPPOSTE Riding east with traffic on the asphalt which was an even surface was better than riding at an angle in the dirt on the side of the road.

ABOVE It was a pleasure to meet Neal Glass, designer and patent holder for the Easyboot, and his wife, Lucille. They flew into Flagstaff to fit Willy with an exact pair of boots. Without them, riding at this pace all day on asphalt and rock, we would not have gotten any farther than Texas.

OPPOSITE Crossing the Colorado River aqueduct that carries water from the Colorado River to agricultural fields and residents in California.

In our case, we needed to change the shoes faster than the hoof wall normally grew out. Fortunately, we had no problem for the first two sets of shoes. But for any shoes thereafter we knew we would not have enough new growth to secure the shoes with new nail holes.

Knowing that this was going to be a problem, our veterinarian, Dr. Hancock, located a company in Santa Fe, New Mexico called Easyboot. It specialized in providing rubber boots as shoes for horses in endurance events. These boots were made of high-impact rubber with clamps that fitted over the horse's steel shoes. Once the boots were clamped on over the hooves, they would last over 800 miles, or four weeks—three times longer than the steel shoes alone were lasting.

This system was very helpful because it allowed the hooves to grow out naturally and the steel shoes acted as a back-up if a horse threw an Easyboot. In this case, we would still have the steel shoes to ride on that day, and then I would simply remove the other three boots so the horse could walk evenly on all four steel shoes.

We had a little powwow with Dr. Hancock and decided to continue riding into Arizona with steel shoes and then fit Willy with Easyboots once we got to Flagstaff. This turned out to be an excellent decision because without them we would not have gotten any farther than Texas. It was also a pleasure to meet Neal Glass (the man who held the patent for the revolutionary "horse boots") and his wife, Lucille, who personally flew into Flagstaff to fit Willy with an exact pair of boots.

As we continued facing new challenges crossing the desert, it became more and more apparent that we didn't have enough team support to maintain the riding pace and do all the other functions needed to keep us on track. Between Sheryl and I, we could barely attend to the horse chores and riding when there were other important tasks to be done. These included trailering to and from the drop off and pick up points, breaking and setting up camp, scouting the route ahead, and attending to the horse chores along with any and all administrative and media work to both keep us on pace and gain us good media exposure.

Fortunately, we got the help we needed, thanks to Al-Marah's Bazy Tankersly. She had already begun recruiting two horse trainers, Brad and Joyce Braden, who had agreed to join our team in Arizona.

The ride through the high desert and down into the Colorado River basin was both bleak and beautiful. Temperatures in the summer can vary in one day by more than 50 degrees. Our route along State Highway 62 was about 75 miles south of Death Valley, the lowest point in America, almost 300 feet below sea level. There were ten lakes along this route, all of which were dry.

The Colorado River aqueduct carries water from the Colorado River to Riverside, California. For a portion of the trip, the aqueduct was parallel to our route. It was a very tempting potential source of water, but we were unable to take advantage of it, as it was fenced on both sides. Our ride in the morning would begin in mid-50s weather and would end

ABOVE The temperature on the asphalt was more than 200 degrees, so soaking Willy's feet in cold water helped dissipate the heat – and then we could pour the warm water on us and the horses.

OPPOSITE (from left to right) Art Parker, Gene Wagner, and Larry Hobbs in front of the Hitchin Post, Twenty Nine Palms, California. They gave us food, water, hay, and grain, and they knew every water stop, rest stop and hook up along the road to Arizona from Twenty Nine Palms. They were a big help but they liked Quarter horses. Oh, well – 9 out of 10 isn't bad.

that same day in 100 degree temperatures. This was early summer in what many call "the most unforgiving environment in America."

On Memorial Day, hundreds of miles from any town, a continuous string of cars coming from L.A. passed Willy and me on the way to the Colorado River. Several people stopped to inquire about our presence in the desert so many miles from cities or towns. I told them about our event and said that I would see them back at the river in June. I was amused to see that even before we reached the river many of the same people were returning two days later. They waved and wished us luck.

Time moves very slowly in the desert, where all is still and waves of heat shimmer off of the asphalt and sand. As it becomes hotter, one can easily fall into a trance, and it is often very difficult to stay awake. Willy and I covered those 250-plus desert miles—often on "automatic pilot." The miles just seemed to drift away, broken up by necessary water stops and a car passing by every 20 or 30 minutes.

Sheryl would drive out into the desert with buckets of water, which we used both to drink and to stand in. The temperature on the asphalt was over 200 degrees and that, combined with the friction of Willy's steel shoes striking asphalt, was a serious concern. To avoid damaging Willy's feet and tendons from the extreme heat buildup, we would place his legs in water buckets to dissipate the heat.

ABOVE Brad and Joyce Braden were horse trainers extraordinaire, but newbies to this ride. Here they are just after they joined the team near the Colorado River. They jumped right in and their contribution was critical to our success.

OPPOSITE The Lower Colorado between Lake Havasu and Parker is a site for many vacationers during Memorial Day. When we encountered them they were incredulous but supportive.

If it was still early morning, we'd quickly see steam come rolling out of the buckets. As soon as the water reached that heat, we'd add new cool water to lower the temperature of Willy's feet and ankles. At these water stops I gratefully doused myself with water, thankful for my long-sleeved shirt and the bandanna over my head, which kept me relatively cool.

We worked our way across the desert in this manner, consuming on any one day over 250 gallons of water among crew, rider, and horse. Thanks to our friends Al Cox, Gene Wagner and Art Parker from The Hitching Post Feed and Tack store in Twenty-Nine Palms, California, our stay in the high desert was much easier. They donated hay and grain, entertained us as we debated the merits of "real" horses (quarter horses) versus Arabians, drove supplies out to us in the desert, gave us a place to stay, and discussed with us every inch of road from Twenty-Nine Palms to the Colorado River.

Best of all, they introduced us to Larry Hobbs. At age 73, Larry rode four hours every day. He had spent thirty years of his life as a rodeo cowboy, during which he was known as "The Cyclone Kid." If Allen Coward was L.A.'s version of the "Man from Snowy River," then watching Larry was like watching the "Man from Snowy River" in a time warp spanning two generations. During the 1950s, Larry had run a ranch that stretched from Skyline Boulevard to Half Moon Bay on the Northern California coast. This ranch was owned by an ex-governor of California, James Rolph, Jr., and Larry spent many hours telling stories about the ranch and the area just north of Monterey Bay.

Larry was tall, lanky, with bright twinkling eyes, sun-baked skin and as close to a caricature of the Sundance Kid as you'd find anywhere. Not surprisingly, we soon found that Larry was as well known for his way with women as he was for his rodeo riding. As Larry described his thirteen wives, "They all wanted a cowboy, but when they got me, they didn't know what to do with me!"

We also learned from Larry that guinea hens made the best watchdogs. "The coyotes can't get close with a guinea hen in the yard," he explained with a grin.

Finally, on June 3rd, we crossed the Colorado River and rode into Parker, Arizona. The couple Mrs. Tankersley had found for us, Brad and Joyce Braden, joined our team along with another trailer and truck. Brad brought a second Al-Marah horse, AM March Along, with him to keep Willy company, and to provide a riding companion for me on some of the lonelier days. Our team was now two horses, one dog, and four people on the road.

We made some strategic decisions and changes during the California segment. One of the most important was to add Brad and Joyce to the ride. Mrs. Tankersley had met Brad at an Arabian event several months before and had told him about our event. Brad's comment at the time was that "it would sure be fun to go along on that ride."

Mrs. Tankersley called him at his Texas home as we were approaching the Arizona border and asked if he and Joyce would like to work with us. They agreed, and ended up helping us in our many horse-related activities and acting as a second or third opinion when talking with our team vet over the phone.

Brad and Joyce were well-known Arabian trainers and ranch managers who'd been involved in the Arabian horse industry for over 35 years. Brad had spent several years in the early 1940s on border patrol, riding 20–30 miles each day along one or more stretches of the United States/Mexico border.

We needed a person on the team with that kind of experience, someone who could offer an experienced second opinion and was familiar with horse-related illness and injury from his day-in, day-out riding. I also often needed a second opinion on the terrain. My first inclination was always to take the shortest and straightest path. Now, armed with Brad's knowledge of terrain and its effect on the team, horse, and riders, we could often pick a more advantageous route.

At the end of the ride that day (June 3rd), Willy and I rode into the Colorado River to cool off as weekend boaters from L.A. zoomed by. Little did I know, as we stood in the cool river, of the adventures awaiting us. We now had one state down and thirteen left to go, but no time to rest on our laurels—there was still a long desert ride ahead to the mountains in northern Arizona, then the Painted Desert and the Indian reservation in northern Arizona. Next, there was a long hot stretch in New Mexico, Texas and Oklahoma.

The thrill of crossing the Colorado was short-lived because I knew I had to prepare myself for the high desert ahead, the vast expanses in Texas and the hot, humid ride through the Midwest.

BELOW One state down, twelve to go. The London Bridge in Lake Havasu is based on the 1831 London Bridge that spanned the River Thames and is clad in the original masonry.

OPPOSITE The day is done and Brad and Sweet William get ready to load up after a 25 mile ride. "Man, am I tired," says the look on Sweet William's face.

ARIZONA

CHAPTER FOUR:
THE PAINTED DESERT AND THE INDIAN RESERVATION

On June 4, 1989, the 17th day of the ride, the new team was moving along the Colorado River on the Arizona side. The elevation was at sea level and we were on State Route 95 heading north for Interstate 40, northern Arizona and the city of Flagstaff, elevation 7,000 feet.

Leaving Flagstaff, our ride would take us up through the Navajo/Hopi Indian reservations and the towns of Ganada and Window Rock. We would then cross the Arizona/New Mexico border and drop down into Gallup, New Mexico. From there, we planned to take Interstate 40 through Albuquerque, and on into Texas.

This was turning out to be one hot stretch. I was consuming about three gallons of water per day and didn't even need to use the bathroom. The horses were drinking about ten buckets of water per day as well.

WARNING
SHALLOW WATER
BOAT TRAFFIC
JUMPING PROHIBITED
LHCC-7-1-19

Grand Canyon

Painted Desert

Window
Rock

FLAGSTAFF

Lake Havasu

PHOENIX

ABOVE This route was hot! During this stretch, the sensation of thirst was central to everything we did, how we planned, and how we rode each day.

OPPOSITE An example of the Letter From The Road that went out twice a month to those we met and those who were following our trip and supporting our efforts. These letters helped us maintain perspective, document the ride, and keep in touch – while the writing was energizing and served as a friendly reminder of our purpose and focus.

Years ago, I had told myself that when I decided to get married, I would take my intended on a cross-country trip in an old car without air conditioning in the summer, coast to coast. If we could make it across the United States in good spirits and still want to be together when we arrived at the opposite coast, then we could probably remain married through anything.

Since the ride, however, I've changed my mind; I'll just take her on a short horseback ride through the Arizona desert.

On this stretch, we were so thirsty we thought about water all the time. The sensation of thirst was central to our very existence. In 1821, the scientist Ruffier said, "Thirst is universally held to be one of the pleasures of life. The sensation cannot be ignored, and if water be lacking, thirst comes to dominate our thoughts and behavior: it drives us to the utmost endeavor and achievement…or to the depths of despair and degradation."

The human body is 65 percent water by weight. Under normal conditions we must replace 1.5 quarts per day of water to survive. While we can go without food for many weeks, we can only go without water for a few days, or sometimes only hours under certain desert conditions.

As we rode along this hot stretch, we got drowsy and often I would daydream.

Willy and I both fell into a trance and cars that went by often had a hypnotic effect on us. The rhythm of those cars whooshing by, together with the steady rocking of our walk, began to play tricks on our minds. One of the hardest tasks was to remain alert. In these situations I would often let my mind wander, and this gave me an opportunity to do a little experiment.

Over a four-day period I wrote down in my journal all of my thoughts, no matter how brief. On June 9th, in a two-hour period, I thought about the following:

- ride logistics, food, water, campsites, fuel, newspaper interviews and a TV interview we had done
- old girlfriends
- high school
- cold water
- the ocean and scuba diving
- how to fix my computer to communicate off of a phone line
- the rainforest
- how little I think about my business

June 14, 1989

LETTER FROM THE ROAD

On May 19, at 6:00 a.m., as dawn was lighting the Pacific surf, Lucian and Willy headed out on the first leg of their long journey. About a half mile from the beach, Lucian and Willy passed several employees coming to work at the power plant along the Santa Ana river. They stopped and asked Lucian, "Where are you riding from?" "The beach" said Lucian. "Where are you going?" With a straight face Lucian replied, "New York." As Lucian and Willy walked on he heard them say, "I think he's serious!" Lucian smiled, Willy snickered.

Hello everyone and welcome back to Ride Across America. So much has happened since we last wrote you, its hard to know where to start. First, thanks to Mary Harris, the owner of the Huntington Beach Equestrian Center for her hospitality, and to Javier who made our life easier in a thousand ways during our stay there. Big hugs to Don Patch and Mary Carpenter and Berniece Toy-Pohlmann who welcomed us like family, loaned Sheryl horses to ride and generally made our stay there the wonderful experience that it was.

On that first day, Lucian and Willy were met about halfway out by Alan Coward and Bob Smith, distance riders from Riverside who helped guide them to our first night's stopping point at Prado Dam. Alan spent many long hours in the saddle and on his motorcycle picking our route for the first three or four days of the trip. There is no question that his support and boundless energy made getting through the concrete jungle not only "doable" as Lucian would say, but safe and enjoyable as well. The only glitch came when Willy, who will walk in the ocean or stand blowing bubbles in a lake, refused to step across a trickle of water, thereby causing Lucian to cross eight lanes of traffic and on another occasion, walk through the parking lot of Anaheim Stadium. Lucian, sitting on Willy, reading his street map and waitng for the light to change, must have been a startling sight for those L.A. commuters at 8:00 a.m. on a Friday morning.

Our other faithful friend for the first part of the trek was Joe Wheatley, a retired Navy pilot from Orange County, who also rode the

RIDE across AMERICA

301 BROADWAY

SUITE A

SAN FRANCISCO CA 94133

(415) 398 4404

him...
nota...

Yucc...
thoug...
until...
the A...
and 30...
Spring...
once g...
of cattl...
man's...
support...
Fox So...
Mountain...
Morongo...
if only L...

Ou...
friends at... ...they donate hay and grain,
Al Cox, ...debating the relative merits of real horses, i.e.
entertain u... ...debating the relative merits of real horses, i.e.
Quarterhorse vs. Arabian, drive supplies to us out in the desert, provide us with a place to stay (thanks Art and Diane) and discuss every stretch of the road from Twenty-Nine Palms to the river, but perhaps best of all they introduced us to Larrry Hobbs.

Seventy-three year old Larry Hobbs, who still rides four to five hours a day, spent thirty years of his life as a rodeo cowboy. During his heyday, he was known as the "Cyclone Kid"-ring any bells? Because it turned out there was no place to pull the rig off the road between Twenty-Nine Palms and Rice, we spent several days at Larry's, trailoring out into the desert and then back at the conclusion of each day's leg. During the 1950's, Larry ran a ranch which stretched from Skyline Blvd. to Half Moon Bay on the Northern Californian coast and was owned by an ex-governor Rolfe, Jr. (California). Sheryl has spent many hours riding and driving those hills just north of Monterey Bay, so his stories were a special treat for her. She narrowly escaped becoming part of the story when Larry proposed that she become wife number fourteen. Said Larry about his thirteen wives, "They all wanted to marry a cowboy, but when they got him they didn't know what to do with him." Before we left Larry took us to his favorite restaurant, an old inn in the high desert that is still a favorite

first leg into Prado and then joined us again through the Morongo Valley and up into Joshua Tree.

On May 20, thirty riders accompanied Lucian and Willy into the lovely Reinhold Arabian Ranch which sits on a bluff overlooking Lake Matthews and the eastern portion of Riverside County. Since our normal starting time is 5:00 a.m., about eight of the riders got up at God knows what hour to meet us at our campsite in a secluded canyon of one of the last of the old ranches, Rancho de la Sierra Vista, to ride the whole leg. Happy days, Eskild Reinhold loaned Sheryl the raffle horse so she got a chance to ride out also, after parking the rig at the Reinhold Ranch. The party that night was wonderful and it was with great reluctance that we headed out the next day. Thanks to the Greater Lake Matthews Trail Association, who organized the party, several thousand dollars were raised for R.A.N.

The next day, who should pop up out of nowhere as Sheryl was knocking on the doors of various dairy farms, but Alan and his wife Melanie. They just wanted to "make sure we were O.K. and that we found a good place to camp." By the way, did you know that the San Jacinto Canyon, through which the Ramona Expressway runs, supports an extensive dairy industry?

The following three days of travel were spent in the shadow of San Jacinto and San Gorgonio Mountains. San Gorgonio is the highest peak to the north of I-10. Its mate, San Jacinto, sits to the south of I-10 right outside Palm Springs. Even the rush of traffic on I-10 did not diminish their presence. San Jacinto in particular, because it sits so close to the highway, seems to sit like a sentinel over the entire valley. And a windy valley it is too! The winds are unrelenting. The natives joke that "this is nothing, sometimes it blows so hard we change zip codes!" Riding from Cabazon up into the town of Morongo Valley, Lucian and Joe Wheatley encountered winds gusting between forty and fifty knots along the ridge where the windmill farms sit. Finally, the last climb up into Yucca Valley and we were in the California high desert.

While scouting that route the day before, Lucian and Joe decided to ...ry and contact the ex-mayor of Palm Springs, Frank Bogert, a long time ...orse enthusiast. A quick visit to the mayor's office at city hall, now ...ccupied by Sonny Bono (yes, of Sonny and Cher fame), and they had ...ank's phone number. After reaching him on our Fujitsu Cellular phone, ...cian and Joe ended up spending several hours with him at his home ...lking about the event. At his request, a number of brochures were left for

...these pledge forms ...receive our Letter From The ... along the way...
...our mailing list. ...mid-west we would like to have several thousand
...ul fundraising, media and logistics.

As you've been reading this Letter From The Road, an area of rainforest the size of metropolitan Los Angeles has been lost to us forever. The tragedy of this loss makes the Ride Across America all the more crucial. With your support we will stop the destruction and save the rainforests.

Lucian   *Lucian*

Sheryl   *[signature]*

Francesca   *Francesca*

...illy   *[signature]*

- mirages and how they appear
- my family and what they were doing
- Willy and how tired he must be
- what Willy must be thinking about
- how tired I was
- pessimism and why so many people are pessimistic
- optimism, are these two traits innate or learned?
- an empty Coke bottle: in the United States, it represents garbage, but in the movie, *The Gods Must Be Crazy*, it represented an opportunity and a host of new ideas
- how important real friends are
- all of the animals that live in the sand on the side of the road whose world is so small, so limited, yet so dangerous. The road is a very dangerous boundary for them, while our world is so large. I concluded that it is all relative.
- how bad we must smell, with no showers in three days
- the temperature in the trailer last night was 109 degrees
- why the desert buzzes
- the only animals I saw during the two hours were a buzzard and a butterfly
- we still have 2,000 plus miles to go
- I must be crazy to run a test like this: It keeps me alert
- wrestling in high school and college and sweating like this to lose weight
- justifying my independence
- how sore my tail is, and if numb means it's getting better or worse
- why am I doing this, really, why?

These were the thoughts I could recall. I documented them during just a two-hour period. It is difficult to believe that you can have so many unrelated thoughts in one hour. Documenting them was difficult, but I found it was very important to let my mind wander, and thus relax.

On the California/Arizona/New Mexico segment, water and all activities related to water were predominant in my thoughts. This ride was as much a mental event as it was a physical event, and perhaps the mental aspect was greater. I found early on that if I worked both my mind and my body, I would quickly drain myself of energy, which I needed to stay motivated and to keep the other team members enthusiastic, too.

Along this stretch, members of the support team began to feel the strain of the ride, and this is where we hit the first wall. Early in the morning of June 13, at 1:00 a.m., Joyce and I took Sheryl to the hospital. She was feeling nauseous and faint, and we found out at the hospital that she was severely dehydrated and suffering from borderline heat stroke (heat prostration) or severe heat exhaustion.

Sheryl was hallucinating, and her fluid level was down so much that it took four liters of fluids and three hours in the hospital to bring her around. The intern on duty told us that this was a very serious matter, that these situations had a way of turning for the worse quickly, and that we had been very smart to respond as we had. He also mentioned that if we had to keep going, we should keep Sheryl out of the sun and keep observing her closely.

The temperature in the trailer that afternoon had been a staggering 133 degrees. Sheryl had not come from a desert climate and was unfamiliar with many of the usual common-sense precautions taken by those who work and play in the sun. For instance, wearing hats, bandannas and long sleeve shirts, seeking shade and drinking water are some of the simple things we can do to keep our bodies properly hydrated.

Because Sheryl wasn't familiar with these precautions, her twelve hours of daily exposure to the sun and her attempts to sleep at night in over 115-degree temperatures had taken their toll.

At the hospital, Joyce told me that earlier that afternoon, Sheryl had decided to go swimming after completing her horse chores. The Colorado River's stretch near our camp was about waist deep, which gave Sheryl a chance to swim and then sit in the river and read. She had spent three hours sitting in the river with only her head exposed and without a hat. The reflection off the water magnified the intense radiation, turning her fair skin and freckles a beet red. From her shoulders up, Sheryl resembled a lobster dipped in boiling water.

Needless to say, Sheryl spent the next two days in the hospital under observation. I shudder to think what might have happened if we had been in a more remote camp without access to emergency services.

Just after our trip to the hospital with Sheryl, she asked us what year it was, if the Colorado River was man-made or natural, and argued that we were riding in the wrong direction, as Las Vegas was south of Arizona. I told her that it was 1989, the Colorado was natural and that all of those gamblers would have had problems placing bets in Spanish.

I knew that the worst was yet to come and that the heat in the Painted Desert, when combined with the long hours and confined living conditions, would only intensify for us under this kind of pace. Day in and day out, the strain continued as the ride wore on, causing tension that could ultimately erupt and jeopardize our chances of reaching our objective.

Sheryl did accompany us to northern Arizona. When we arrived at the Al-Marah Hat Ranch, the physical toll on us all having just ridden thru some of the hottest desert in the west was very obvious to the ranch management. After assessing the physical requirement ahead for us, the Al-Marah team decided to reassign Sheryl to other activities within their organization.

She left the ride in Northern Arizona to recover, and after a short rest moved down to southern Arizona to begin working at the Al-Marah Ranch in Tucson. We felt better knowing she would no longer be exposed to the harsh conditions that lay ahead.

On June 11, Brad was riding March Along and I was riding Willy. We crossed the London Bridge, which had actually been shipped over from London, England, piece by piece, bricks, lamp posts, etc., all in original condition. It had been put back together here in Lake Havasu City, Arizona, as a tourist attraction.

On June 12 at 11:00 a.m., it was already hot on State Route 95 heading north to Interstate 40 east. A man in a Cadillac passed us; then, he braked, made a U-turn, pulled up next to us and rolled down his window.

"What are you doing on that horse?" the driver asked.

"I'm riding him to New York City to raise money for the rainforest," I replied.

The man motioned me closer. As I leaned over in the saddle to look inside his car, he flipped a switch that displayed the outside temperature on his dashboard. "You damn fool— it's 117 degrees out there!" His car's electric window zipped up as he made another U-turn and sped on down the highway. That night, we found ourselves on the front page of the local paper and received a far more friendly response the next day along the highway. Many people stopped their cars to chat and ask us how they could help.

Each evening in camp we set up a table with pledge forms and information on the rainforest. I passed out brochures along the way, and those who read the articles in the local papers or saw us along the road stopped by our camp in the evening and talked to us. I was usually in bed by 7:00 p.m., exhausted.

As we worked our way through the mountains of northern Arizona, we found the temperatures were much cooler, especially when we reached an elevation of 3,500 feet. We were moving steadily along Interstate 40, where we could ride off the interstate parallel to the fence line that bordered this area. As we picked our way along the fence line through volcanic rock, juniper and cactus, I noticed that Willy was beginning to act very strangely. His ears were at full attention and his neck snaked out as he sniffed the wind and ground ahead.

We were approaching a very large juniper tree with branches that hung down to the ground and Willy snorted, his nostrils flaring, and he sucked in great amounts of air. We were obviously up-wind of something. As we continued to inch forward I heard low snarls, as did Willy. We both had the same idea at the same time—get the heck out of there!

As I leaned to the right, Willy turned to the left and several coyotes exploded from the juniper tree, dragging a very large carcass. We were now about four feet from the tree, and in the confusion I lost a stirrup, but managed to stay in the saddle. The coyotes, however, weren't willing to give up any ground, and stared at us as they stood over their meal. We left them with the carcass, retracing our steps along the fence line.

During this stretch across northern Arizona, we made a base camp at the Hat Ranch. The ranch belonged to Mrs. Bazy Tankersley and rests on 125,000 acres of Forest Service land with elk, bear, antelope, cows and horses. It was a welcome break from the heat in western Arizona. The ranch was basically unchanged from the late 1800s, but today, Mrs. Tankersley does have a phone and a generator and solar power. This ranch and other ranches like it form part of a very large watershed, where small tributaries in these and other mountains combine as they flow south into the drainage basin and ultimately to Phoenix and California.

Here's a bit of history. In 1934, Arizona and California were at odds with one another over Colorado River water rights. In 1944, this was further complicated by an agreement between the United States and Mexico that mandated the United States provide Mexico with 500,000 "acre feet of water" each year from this river. (An acre foot of water is the amount of water that covers one acre, one foot deep). This is lot of water, and now, in the twenty-first century, we are still having problems meeting our requirement.

As the water from the Colorado flows south toward Mexico, it becomes saltier; the concentration of salt as the water evaporates becomes higher in the remaining water. What causes this? Primarily, it's human consumption of water. When we remove water from the river, we leave behind the salt and chemicals from that water. We also construct dams and reservoirs along the river, causing the salt and chemicals to collect.

All this salt has become a major concern as the Colorado River flows into northern Mexico and the Sea of Cortez, often known as the Gulf of California. This saltwater body

This would not be the last time that Willy and Lucian had a difference of opinion on which way to turn. However, the coyotes win this standoff.

needs fresh water; and there is not much fresh water from the river emptying into the sea, which makes the whole northern Baja area saltier. This increase in salinity affects the balance of nature in this region through the food chain of plants and animals that rely on water of a certain level of salinity. As a result, some plants and animals can no longer live in the northern region on this sea, and in turn Mexico's fishing industry is adversely affected.

At this point in the ride we had covered 800 miles and were now 27 percent of the way across the United States. We had been on the road for 60 days. During this same time, at the then current rate of deforestation, the planet lost over 300,000 acres of rainforest and several hundred species of unknown and undocumented plants and animals. Unfortunately, these were lost forever.

Because the Arizona Department of Transportation did not give us permits for a stretch of Interstate 40 from Flagstaff to the New Mexico border, we had to ride up through northeastern Arizona and the Navajo/Hopi Indian reservations. Now, looking back, I'm glad we did ride through "The Res," as locals called this area. Physically, it hadn't changed much over the past hundred years.

The country was beautiful but bleak, empty and desolate. There was no electricity or running water and very few towns to be found. A crossroad might have a gas station and a convenience store, but any real clothes or food shopping required the Navajos to travel 200 miles or more—one way!

On the reservation, we set up a pretty primitive camp. Because we had hay and feed in our trucks and water in our storage tanks, we became a midnight attraction for many of the wild horses and cows in the vicinity. Each evening we were visited by these very aggressive animals, which made Willy and March Along very nervous. The visitors would snort and kick outside our trucks in their attempts to get to the supplies inside.

In response, we would alternate standing guard over our camp and taking turns chasing the wild stock away. This would go on all night until daybreak. Finally, I spoke to the locals about this. They said they were going to round up all the stray cows and horses with no brands on them. These would be shot and sent to Flagstaff to be butchered, as there just wasn't enough water or forage to go around that summer.

On the reservation, water rationing was a problem so we often went without showers, using the available water for drinking and cooking only. The horses came first and the human team members second. In Ganado, Arizona, for seven evenings we made trips to the fire station to fill up our water tanks and make our phone calls. In 1989, there was only one public pay phone and the population of less than 500 was limited to 75 gallons of water in the morning and 75 gallons in the evening.

That supplied two horses and three people with just enough water per day. The people on the reservation did this every day of the summer. By contrast, on an average day an

OPPOSITE The original ranch house for Bazy's Hat Ranch in northern Arizona. This ranch has been host to two United States Presidents over the years – Teddy Roosevelt and Franklin Roosevelt. Bazy likes to call this her "equine outward bound program" where the horses are allowed to run together in a larger herd so they can learn to fend for themselves, socialize with one another, and grow strong legs and hooves as they canter through the rough terrain.

American family of four cooking, washing clothes and dishes, bathing and flushing the toilet can consume 500 gallons of water per day.

About halfway through the Navajo reservation, as we rode along a lonely stretch of road, I happened upon a 16-year-old girl who was walking home. I had not seen a car in over an hour and I was more than a 20-hour ride from the nearest town. I saw no towns or houses on the horizon. When I asked her where she lived, she pointed at the horizon to a ridge of low mountains at least 40 miles away. We were walking along together at about the same pace, so I got off and put the duffle bag she was carrying on Willy. It was heavier than Willy's saddle, at least 70 pounds, and must have been very heavy for a 16-year-old girl to carry on a hot day for a long hike.

As we walked along, I found out that her name was Tammy and that she had been in a drug rehab program in Flagstaff. The program was over and she was free to go home for a few days. The problem was getting there; she had no ride and her mother had no car. She wanted to see her grandmother, who lived on the reservation, because Tammy felt that she still carried within her an addiction to drugs. Her grandmother had told her she would work with the medicine man to help rid her of these spirits. Tammy spoke with a speech impediment, which she said was a result of a drug overdose.

She had been a cross-country runner before she got involved in drugs and told me she wanted to start running again when her body and mind were no longer "dreaming of drugs." I told her I, too, used to run cross-country in high school. We walked together for about ten miles. Then she turned to me and said that her trail was over the next ridge, and that she must turn off the road to follow it east.

As we topped the ridge, I expected to see a road or at least a two-lane truck trail, but nothing marked the spot. I asked again with what must have been an incredulous look on my face: "Are you sure this is where you get off?" It was empty, simply desert and mountains, no sign of people.

"Yes," she confirmed, but I saw she had no water, so I filled up her plastic jug with the rest of mine. I knew Brad would be along within the next two hours, as I could now tell time by the sun and my shadow. Tammy gave me some fry bread in return, waved goodbye and walked off into the desert. Within minutes I could no longer see her…and I never saw her again.

I continued to have strange experiences on the reservation. On July 2, I was riding along a stretch of dirt road with no signs of human activity. I knew from the maps that we were about 15 miles from the nearest crossroad. This dirt road was a shortcut that I had spotted several days before, but had not scouted out the route, so we were riding blind. I had told Brad to meet me at a specific location on the other side of this mountain at a specific time.

As we climbed into the mountains, there were many small roads branching off; I kept to the most worn of these roads, hoping that we would eventually end up back on the main road in time to meet Brad. From my vantage point, I could see about 50 miles in every direction as our path dropped down into a large valley.

ABOVE and OPPOSITE The Navajo Nation reservation in Northern Arizona is a territory covering 26,000 square miles and is the largest land area assigned primarily to a Native American jurisdiction within the U.S. Sheep and horses were brought to North America and the southwest by the Spanish and by the eighteenth century, the Navajo had herds of horses which they considered as sacred, and no different from family.

As we got to the bottom, I heard a shrill whinny to our left. Having already encountered wild cattle and horses, I didn't want another encounter in the middle of nowhere and I didn't want to canter on down the road because that would draw more attention and possibly cause the group of horses to chase us. When horses meet one another, they often kick and bite to establish a pecking order. This is usually okay when the horses are not encumbered with a saddle and rider, but Willy was at a disadvantage and I didn't want either of us to get hurt.

One minute later, I saw a dust storm rolling toward us off the ridge. In front of it was a group of horses running full tilt directly at us! Willy was prancing in circles and I was doing everything I could do to hold him back, not knowing if he wanted to run or fight. I was determined to stand our ground because I knew we would tire too easily in an all-out sprint. It was late in the day and we were 18 miles into a 24-mile day, with a temperature of 104°F. We were tired but I hoped we could bluff the horses if we stood our ground. They were now about a football field away and going full out, six of them, all different colors.

Willy was all over the place, and I had to keep him prancing in circles to keep him in place. The lead horse was red, with a screaming whinny. There was a white horse running next to him, stride for stride, but this horse was quiet. Then, just as they were closing in on us, Willy suddenly stopped prancing, turned to face the oncoming horses, planted his feet wide apart and stood very still and steady, not shaking, but I could feel his tension.

The red horse stopped and snorted, and the other horses stopped in a cloud of dust, milling behind the lead horse. This whole encounter took just about three minutes.

It was a standoff. Bluffing confidence, I clicked a knee into Willy to square him off to the lead red horse. We were about 20 feet apart, close enough for the red horse to reel and kick us. Not seeing any brands, halters or ropes on these horses, I thought they might be wild. The red horse was flaring his nostrils and bobbing his head up and down, snaking it around as if he were trying to get a sniff of us.

This went on for about 30 seconds, with the wild horses stamping and snorting. I did not want to add an unknown variable to this drama, so I said nothing. About a minute went by in the standoff, with the other five horses milling around behind the red horse. Willy and I stood our ground, becoming more and more confident every second.

Suddenly, I realized that the red horse was blind! In fact, he was cleverly using the white horse as his lead! How had he run so smoothly across the desert toward us? I waved my hand and he didn't follow my movement. He did, however, react to my voice, nipping the white horse next to him. They trotted off in rhythm, leading the other four horses with them. For the next hour, they shadowed us at a distance. Then they just disappeared into a juniper forest.

I looked down at Willy's shoulders, now covered with white lather. As for me, I was drenched in sweat, too.

A three-legged horse: mirage or reality? On the same day at the end of that ride, I was on a two-lane road riding toward the spot where Brad and I had agreed to meet. There

were fences on both sides of the road, and red clay, low sage, and cactus for miles to my left and right.

I saw a small hut up on the mountain to my right. It was still very far away but I could see some people moving around it and some horses in front. To my left were some cattle moving, maybe a mile out in the desert. As I rode down this road, I saw the people to my right saddle up—two people and three horses. They seemed to be leading one horse.

As they began riding toward the road, I thought that I would have to trot to meet them as they crossed the road. They were still very far away and moving faster than we were. When they got to the road, they were about half mile ahead of us. Then, they disappeared and reappeared on the other side of the road, now to my left, riding toward the cattle.

That was hardly unusual; they were probably going over to herd the cattle to another part of the range and had gone under the road through a drainage tunnel or culvert. As I got closer and saw them continue to move farther to my left into the open range, I noticed the third horse was not on a lead. He was limping as though he were lame, and the closer I got, the more evident the limp.

When they were about 100 yards to my left and heading straight off my left shoulder, I noticed the last horse only had three legs. This third horse would stop, then trot, then hop as it tried to keep up with the other two.

Willy and Lucian encounter the blind red horse.

Controversy surrounds the presence of Mustang herds. Supporters argue that Mustangs are part of the natural heritage of the West and they have an inherent right of inhabitation while others argue that they degrade rangeland and compete with livestock and wild species for forage. Most Mustangs live in arid areas that cattle cannot fully utilize as they are better adapted by evolution to such climates, traveling as much as 50 miles a day, allowing them to utilize areas not grazed by cattle.

I stopped Willy to watch this very strange procession move on after the cattle. It seemed as if the second rider might be the son and the first rider the father. The son kept waiting for the three-legged horse to catch up. By the time they got to the cattle they were very far away from us. They appeared to be bringing the cattle into a very tight circle and then kept riding right up into the mountains, the third horse dragging behind on three legs.

I was very disturbed by the sight and thought, "How cruel, bringing a three-legged horse on a trail ride."

When I passed this story on to the other people on the team that evening, they thought I had been out in the sun too long. I swore up and down that I had seen a three-legged horse that day. Nobody believed me. Someday I am going to go back up onto that reservation and find that hut and that rancher and ask him if he actually had a horse with three legs.

Just as we began crossing the Indian reservation, I got a note from my brother, John. He was sending me the lyrics from a song from the seventies by the group, *America,* and it perfectly described my present situation.

ABOVE America's "A Horse with No Name" was originally called "Desert Song" and was written to capture the feel of the hot, dry desert, which had been depicted on the wall at America's recording studio. Song writer Dewey Bunnell also said that this song reminded him of his childhood travels through the Arizona desert when his family lived at Vandenberg Air Force Base. (Lyrics by Dewey Bunnell, ©1971)

OPPOSITE A View of the Painted Desert

On the first part of the journey,
I was looking at all the life.
There were plants and birds. and rocks and things,
There was sand and hills and rings.
The first thing I met, was a fly with a buzz,
And the sky, with no clouds.
The heat was hot, and the ground was dry,
But the air was full of sound.

I've been through the desert on a horse with no name,
It felt good to be out of the rain.
In the desert you can remember your name,
'Cause there ain't no one for to give you no pain.
La, la, la la la la, la la la, la, la
La, la, la la la la, la la la, la, la

After nine days, I let the horse run free,
'Cause the desert had turned to sea.
There were plants and birds, and rocks and things,
There was sand and hills and rings.
The ocean is a desert, with its life underground,
And a perfect disguise above.
Under the cities lies, a heart made of ground,
But the humans will give no love.

You see I've been through the desert on a horse with no name,
It felt good to be out of the rain.
In the desert you can remember your name,
'Cause there ain't no one for to give you no pain.
La la, la, la la la la, la la la, la, la
La la, la, la la la la, la la la, la, la

I found myself humming that song non-stop. It would be my constant companion on our journey.

NEW MEXICO AND TEXAS

CHAPTER FIVE:
THE PREACHER AND THE BLUE HOLE

BELOW Old Route 66 served us well as we rode bits and pieces of this now historic road as it sometimes ran parallel to our "straight as a string" route. Riding Route 66 was scenic and more interesting and provided us with a great opportunity to connect with more people and talk about the rainforest as we rode through many small towns.

We crossed into New Mexico on July 4th. Country star Waylon Jennings was playing in concert on the reservation in Window Rock, Arizona, just west of the Arizona/New Mexico border. I rode by the concert hall on our way through town and would have liked to attend, but the concert was sold out five days after tickets went on sale. I thought that this was an interesting, if rather out of the way place to play in concert on the Fourth of July.

Crossing into New Mexico was significant for a number of reasons. We were just shy of being one-third of the way across the United States, and we were now in another time zone, adding one hour as we crossed into New Mexico. You might think that at the pace we were traveling one hour would not make a difference, but it did, especially in the early morning. We could now set the clock one hour later and still be on the road before daybreak. It took us several days to adjust to the new schedule.

GALLUP

ALBUQUERQUE

SANTA ROSA

Rio
Grande

BELOW Bob and Bea Shepard standing in front of
their "house on wheels." They were intrigued by the
event and joined up with the team in Gallup, New
Mexico, at the KOA Campground, after first watching
the "lunging" demonstration and listening to onlookers
who were asking questions about the rainforest.

When we reached Gallup, New Mexico the first week of July, we stayed at a KOA
campground. After our ride that afternoon, I spent about two hours talking with the KOA
manager and his wife about our event and the rainforests. They were so interested in our event
that they offered to let us stay for three days "on the house." We gave them a T-shirt and a
video about our journey.

July 6th was a rest day, so I spent the day working with Brad on our route. We'd be
riding through Gallup, on Old Route 66 and then farther along Interstate 40. Later that day, I
spoke with local city officials and the local paper about why we were making the ride. I did
two radio interviews and a television interview, which we saw on the 6:00 p.m. news. This
was very good publicity for the manager of the KOA campground, too, who offered us an
extended stay if we wished. We took him up on his generous offer.

We now had rooms, time, and plenty of water, enough that we could give both horses
a warm water bath. What a contrast to only two days before on the reservation, when we had
just enough water to cook with and to keep the horses going.

Joyce and Brad gave both horses a long, hot bath and even put some conditioner in their
manes and tails. This exercise attracted quite a bit of attention in the campground from both
children and adults, and when Brad started lunging Willy, a crowd gathered to watch.

"Lunging" a horse means that you tie a 30-foot long rope to the horse's halter and let
him travel in circles, first at a walk, then at a trot, and then at a canter. Brad was very good at
controlling the horse with verbal cues, so Willy would canter and stop on Brad's command,
then turn and go in the opposite direction. Willy was on Brad's lunge line and Joyce had March
Along on the other, the horses were now going in opposite directions right next to each other.
Both horses were clean and had their tails up and ears forward, prancing like show horses.

After we were done and the crowd had dispersed, a man walked up to Brad and
introduced himself. They spoke for a while, and then he invited us over to his trailer for a
snack and a cold drink.

The man was Bob Shepard. He and his wife, Bea, were originally from Connecticut. As
a result of some very good business opportunities, Bob had retired very early and had been
on the road for a year. He and Bea had traveled all around the United States. At the time we
met, they were in Gallup headed east along the same route we were traveling. They literally
lived in a high-tech house on wheels, and I was very impressed with their video and camera
equipment, the computers and the satellite dish on top of their Winnebago.

Then, an idea popped into my mind. We had made an agreement with Channel 9 News in Tucson to send back video and TV spots along the way. In return, every Thursday on the evening news, they would show an image of a horse and rider on the weather map as we made our way across the United States. This would let our friends, family and the people at Al-Marah follow our progress.

Every once in a while, I could convince a local TV station along the route to send in its piece to Channel 9. When this generated quite a bit of interest in Tucson, the station asked me whether we could send them some video each week, along with our location and a phone interview. While I couldn't get actual TV footage from local stations along the way, Channel 9 was willing to accept a video. However, we had no video equipment with us, so thus far, there had been disappointment all around.

But after I saw Bob's equipment that evening, I told him the story about the TV station, and he offered to do a short video for us the next morning. We later found that Bob and Bea were actually professional camera people!

We often tried to set up our interviews with the local media in a natural setting like this park in downtown Albuquerque, New Mexico.

ABOVE The central theme of the Kachina culture is the presence of life in all objects that fill the universe. Everything has an essence or a life force, and humans must interact with these or fail to survive. We thought this was an appropriate perspective for our ride.

OPPOSITE Interstate 40 outside of Albuquerque was barren but beautiful with red rock bluffs on both sides of the highway.

The following evening as we sat in the Shepards' house on wheels, Bob showed us our whole day's ride on video. It was amazingly well done and very creative. He had arisen in the early morning and done the early part of the video in the dark with lights, and then filmed us off and on throughout the day.

I promptly asked him if we could send the video to Tucson and he replied, "No problem" and offered to travel with us to document the event on film. He didn't simply mean for the next couple of days—he meant for the rest of the trip. And we still had three months to go! I happily agreed to bring them aboard.

While we were riding through the reservation in Northern Arizona, Bob and Bea were there as well, visiting with several of the tribe's artists in some of the more remote areas of the reservation. The couple had developed a fascination with Indian Kachina dolls and spent quite a bit of time and money looking for originals. The central theme of the Navajo and Kachina culture is the presence of life in all objects that fill the universe. Everything has an essence or a life force, and humans must interact with these or fail to survive.

When I think of Bob and Bea, I will always think of Kachina dolls. We became very good friends over the course of this ride as I began to bounce problems and ideas off them. Bob began to work with Brad on the route logistics, while Bea joined with Bob to set up interviews along the road and clear our route through the towns we would pass through.

Bob also began working more and more with Francesca of the Rainforest Action Network to coordinate our route and other logistics while I was on the horse each day. This all took a lot of pressure off Brad and me. We quickly integrated Bob and Bea into the team as we all began to assume more specific tasks. Brad and Joyce continued with the horse chores, breaking and setting up camp, scouting the terrain and the route and managing the pick-ups and drop-offs each day. This allowed Bob and Bea to assume handling of all of the media events, contacting the local press and setting up the various interviews before, during, and after each day's ride.

This left me with the riding and the interviews. The additional administrative bandwidth and expertise that Bob and Bea brought to the table was both much needed and timely and allowed us to get more done daily than before.

Just east of Gallup was a small row of houses and farms. As I rode through this area, I saw two open-air churches. They looked more like podiums covered with sheet metal roofs in a cathedral arch, with rows and rows of chairs facing the podium.

I thought, "How uncomfortable that would be in the winter," and as I rode past the facilities, I wished I could see a congregation sitting in the chairs listening to someone speaking at the podium. It was early on a Monday morning, so I was amazed when around the next corner I actually heard a minister! As we rounded the bend, he was saying, "These kids nowadays have no common sense, no horse sense." Just as he said the words, "horse sense," Willy let out a loud, shrill whinny.

The minister stopped talking as the whole congregation turned around and stared. We were only about 75 feet from the outdoor church, and I was laughing and pointing at Willy. I shrugged my shoulders as if to say, "Hey, that wasn't my idea!"

The timing was impeccable. I looked around and saw no other horses around that might have made Willy react with a whinny, so I just chalked it up to the fact that Willy had overheard the preacher and was disagreeing with him. It was quite bizarre, as Willy was not very vocal as horses go and this was the first time he had done anything like this. He did this only one other time during the ride.

We moved our camp to Grants, New Mexico, about halfway between Gallup and Albuquerque. This area of New Mexico is desolate but beautiful, with immense red rock bluffs overlooking the desert straddling both sides of the highway. We had an exceedingly beautiful section to ride through that afternoon and the area made a spectacular backdrop for a picture.

Louise Serpa, a photographer from Santa Fe, came down and shot several rolls in the mountains along the highway. For these shots, I rode in cowboy boots and wore Brad's cowboy hat (not my usual attire) because we needed some props for these shots. Afterward, I quickly changed back into my Nike shoes and running outfit.

If you have to do any walking in the desert, you don't want to be encumbered with cowboy boots. My choice of attire was most appropriate for this ride. I know because the one time Brad got his truck stuck in the desert back in Arizona, he had walked about one mile in his cowboy boots and suffered with painful blisters for a week.

Of course, if I wanted to do any hiking or climbing and was leading Willy, I had to do it in shoes I could maneuver in. But for the sake of these PR shots, the cowboy attire was the most appropriate.

A fund-raiser in Santa Fe at Leslie Barclay's place was our first one since Flagstaff, three weeks earlier. Leslie was on the board of advisors for the ride. She had been instrumental in our success thus far and had a real interest in this event. For this fund-raiser, she sent out more than 200 invitations, and about 120 turned out for dinner and a video about the ride.

Afterward, we spent two days in Santa Fe doing interviews and resting. Then we took the trailer back down to Albuquerque and our base camp along the route.

In Albuquerque, we rode through town at midnight along Old State Route 66. We found out at the end of the ride that day that the third shift police captain was a rider and had told his officers that he wanted to be sure we had no trouble as we rode through town. Police cars shadowed us the whole way, clearing the alleys and streets well in advance of our arrival. It was great!

It didn't last, however. Later, we were stopped seven times in a one-hour stretch along the highway just east of Albuquerque. Officers from three different precincts and two different agencies were astounded when they found out we had a permit to ride along the interstate in New Mexico. A permit like this had never been issued prior to our ride. I finally began taping my permit to the saddle like a license plate. When the next two officers stopped

ABOVE 11:00 p.m., saddling up for a night ride.

OPPOSITE Getting ready for the night rides was always more difficult than doing the ride. Lucian and Willy in downtown Albuquerque at 1:30 a.m.

In 1539, Francisco Coronado, who was the Governor of New Spain, funded an expedition to find Cibola (one of the Seven Cities of Gold) in what is now known as Arizona and New Mexico. In 1542, while in New Mexico, he was injured in a fall from his horse and returned to his estate in Mexico.

ABOVE Lucian (on the right) and a student in a deep dive at 90 feet, struggling to surface a whale vertebrae from the whale grave yard off San Pedro Island in the Sea of Cortez, Mexico.

OPPOSITE While the landscape around Santa Rosa is semi-arid ranch country, Santa Rosa is scuba diving heaven. The Blue Hole is 90 feet deep, with clean, clear, cold water – and just waiting for Lucian to dive in.

us, I simply pointed to my license plate. They detained us for a short time, and then let us go on our way.

Francesca and Bob had set up an interview session with the local media in Albuquerque at the Rio Grande Nature Center. This natural park, with very few trails, was enough to confuse half of the media people who tried to show up. We thought it would be a good idea to have our press conference at this beautiful location that would make a good setting for a photo shoot. The press conference produced three newspaper interviews, plus spots on two TV stations and one radio station. Several other media groups got lost trying to find the park, and those who did could not follow our directions or find the right trail.

Needless to say, all of our future interviews would be held in well-known locations. After this last interview session, Bob scheduled a Rotary meeting for us to attend so I could get a chance to speak with about 300 local businessmen. That was a full day and then back to camp and bed.

Riding into Santa Rosa, I crossed the Pecos River. In 1540, that river had quite a lot of water flowing through it and the small plaque on the two lane bridge said: "Francisco Coronado camped here for four days in 1540. He built a wooden bridge across the Pecos River: Coronado was looking for Cibola and its cities of gold. Coronado went on into Kansas from here."

Santa Rosa was a small town of about 2,500 people, several RV parks and quite a few hotels and restaurants. Because of its distance from Albuquerque, it received business from truck drivers along the interstate. Santa Rosa also had a Rotary Club that Bob attended, speaking to the members about the ride and the rainforest issue. As a result, word spread quickly and we had several visitors at the campground and along the route.

Santa Rosa was also the home of the "Blue Hole." I could not resist—I had been riding past these signs for several days and I was intrigued. Imagine a scuba diving spot in the middle of this desert-like area! After our ride that afternoon, Bob and Bea and I went to the "Blue Hole." We were all very impressed with this large spring: thousands of gallons of cold, clear water poured out of this hole in the ground every second.

There were several scuba divers down in the spring. I was told the bottom was about 90 feet down, but that there was a false bottom at about 60 feet. I wanted to take a look and felt confident that I could get down about 60 feet. I had been a scuba instructor and had done quite a bit of free diving—I could hold my breath for over two minutes and dive down to 60 feet.

I always taught my new students the art of "buddy breathing" on their first couple of dives, letting them swim around for 15 or 20 minutes in about 40 or 50 feet of water. Then I would free-dive in with no tank and ask one of the students for air. This would always catch them by surprise and would take them a second or so to respond. I could buddy breathe till I saw another student maybe 30 or 40 feet away and then I would leave and swim over to that student. I could spend 10 or 12 minutes under water without tanks, swimming from student to student.

It was great practice for me and not dangerous at all. If I couldn't reach a student, I would simply go to the surface. For the students, it was great training because when I did

reach them, I was desperately in need of air. Under actual conditions, they learned what it meant to "buddy breathe."

In this case, I thought I could dive down to the false bottom at about 60 feet, find a diver, ask for air, and stick around long enough to check out the bottom. I always got a kick out of seeing the expression on a person's face when I swam up in 60 feet of water with no tank and gave the universal sign that I needed air. My only concern was that several years prior, during an emergency rescue, I suffered a debilitating over-pressurization injury to my inner ear. In essence, I blew my eardrum and fractured a bone in the round window of my inner ear. As a result, I lost 30 percent of my hearing in my right ear.

That accident cut my diving career short. Since then I had dived only twice, both times against the recommendations of my doctor. Both times were in warm shallow water and with tanks. But it had been more than three years since my last dive and over six years since the injury. I now concluded that I should be able to do a deep free-dive with no problem and that my ear was probably strong enough to take it.

At about 20 feet down, I stopped to equalize. Holding my nose, I exhaled a bit of air and then, boom! I blew out my eardrum again! Cold water rushed into my inner ear and caused me to lose my sense of balance. As a result, I became very nauseous. With this loss of balance came a loss of direction.

In situations like these, some divers can't even find the surface. When you have tanks on, even with the extreme pain, you are taught to watch your bubbles and you know where the surface is. In a free dive you don't have these bubbles, as you are holding your breath. The pain is excruciating. Luckily, having been in this situation before, despite the pain, I did not lose my wits, got the situation under control and found the surface.

Bob and Bea took me straight to a local doctor, who cleaned some of the blood out of my ear. The doctor described the rupture as a medium-size tear and suggested I take some antibiotics and stay out of the water until the tear healed. As his contribution to the ride, the doctor did not charge us for the visit or the antibiotics.

I was still in pain and very nauseous, and once back in camp I went to bed at about 2:00 p.m. for a 3:30 a.m. wake-up call the next morning. What I had thought would be a way to unwind really backfired. Live and learn!

I spent the next few days riding and recovering from my run-in at the "Blue Hole." We were making very good time and were all in pretty good spirits. We were now in a town called Tucumcari, New Mexico. Joyce and Bea had been in town earlier to do some shopping and had found several good stores for antiques. Joyce bought an old typewriter for her journal and Bea bought some groceries. I was going into town myself to deliver some mail and do some shopping for food. I also wanted to find a good restaurant for us for dinner later that evening. I dropped off the mail and went on to the local grocery store.

While standing at the copy machine, five cents a copy, a local 25-year-old, more than a little inebriated, walked up and said to me, "We don't like your kind around here." I stood there a second and asked myself what it was that he didn't like. My clothes didn't fit the bill locally and my bright orange bike hat did stand out—but I guessed it was the running tights.

I was still pretty burned out from the ride that day and still wearing my grimy riding clothes, but I wasn't talking to anyone or doing any interviews, so I hadn't seen any need to change. I was just trying to blend in, but was obviously not succeeding.

I quickly realized that the young man and his friend were bound and determined to make this confrontation a point. Now I'm not a real big person and don't weigh much, but I am quick. In this case, my agility put me at somewhat of an advantage. I turned slowly from the copy machine and walked up as close as I could get and asked him what, specifically, it was that he didn't like. That seemed to confuse him.

Many birds that spend the summer in North American back yards migrate to tropical rainforests in the winter. The Baltimore oriole travels from the United States, more than 3,000 miles to winter in the warm forests of Central and South America. In Texas, each year, more than 250 species of small songbirds, among them warblers, orioles and tanagers, migrate from Central and South America to become temporary Texans. These birds serve a dual purpose as they help pollinate crops and other plants in the U.S. and as they feed they help keep the insect population under control as well.

Canadian
River

AMARILLO

OPPOSITE The clean highway program, started by Lady Bird Johnson, made riding along the highways in Texas a real pleasure. Amarillo is also a real horse town and for this reason we got great media coverage. Bob even did his first presentation on the rainforest to a friendly audience of local business leaders. With the largest meat packing facility in the U.S. and large ranches everywhere, Amarillo is a cattle marketing and economic center for the Texas Panhandle.

At this point several people stopped to watch. Just as he was getting ready to respond, he lost his balance and fell backward over the mop display at the head of this particular aisle. His companion watched and said nothing. The manager of the store came over to apologize to me and then led both men out of the store.

I finished making the copies and, as I was leaving, asked one of the check-out clerks at the register whether she could recommend any good restaurants. "Are you packin'?" she asked.

"No," I said.

"That leaves only the Holiday Inn and the motel next door. After that incident you'd best be packin' around here. Word spreads fast."

Later that evening we all went to the Holiday Inn and played pool. Brad and Joyce and Bob and Bea did some dancing and I watched. We sat and talked about the incident at the local Safeway. Just as we were talking, two more somewhat inebriated tough guys (who obviously heard about the Safeway scene) showed up at our table. These guys were out to harass us some more.

As we began talking to our newest tough guys, we learned that they were brothers of the guy I had pushed over the mop display earlier in the day. We tried to exit the bar quietly, but they kept poking at us with their pool cues.

Luckily, while Brad and I were trying to figure out how to manage the pending confrontation, in walked the sheriff, and not a moment too soon. I was seconds away from grabbing the pool cue the guy was wielding when apparently the bartender, who sensed this and was afraid this situation was going in the wrong direction, called the sheriff, who had actually read the front page article about our ride. When he heard that we'd had a brief altercation at the Safeway, and then were in over our heads at the local bar, he quickly came to our rescue.

Brad got out the camera and started shooting as we were asked by the sheriff for our autograph, as well as a photo with our team and the horses in front of the Sheriff's office. So all things considered, we left in very good shape!

On day sixty-seven, July 24th, I was riding through Amarillo, Texas, when a film crew came out in the early morning to film Willy and me for the evening news. The reporter asked me several questions about the ride and the purpose behind it. At the end of the interview he asked the most important question: "What impact does deforestation in the rainforest have on Amarillo, Texas, and on this area?"

This question reflected what people there were asking themselves as we were riding through, and I wanted my answer to bring home their connection with this global issue. So I answered, "Deforestation and loss of rainforests has an impact on global climate patterns and the migratory species that pollinate crops. This has a long-term effect on the panhandle of Texas, the Midwest and other areas of the United States."

Because people in this area needed rain desperately, as well as pollinators to grow their crops, the point struck home!

Man riding horse cross country to boost awareness of rain forests

By AMY BOARDMAN
Globe-News Staff Writer

After being on horseback almost continuously for more than three months, it would seem that Lucian Spataro might be growing a little tired of cheerleading the cause he's been pitching for the last 1,500 miles.

But, with another 1,500 miles to go, Spataro, of Tuscon, Ariz., isn't about to slow down until he's increased the country's awareness of a seemingly unlikely cause for the 31-year-old horseman: rain forests.

"It's the ecosystem we're losing the quickest," Spataro said of the forests that cover about 2 percent of the Earth's surface. "If you don't have an environment, who cares about the rest? It's the basis of everything we do. AIDS and homelessness ceases to be a problem if you have no ecosystem."

Spataro, a member of the San Francisco-based Rainforest Action Network, has ridden about 22 —
May 19, when h—

shouting distance about rain forests.

Spataro and company probably reach about 50 people a day just by riding through small towns and at the trailer parks they stop at every night, he said. By the time they reach New York, Spataro estimates he will have talked to several thousand people about the forests.

"It's a real grass-roots approach to generate interest, but it's probably the best way," he said.

The increasingly rapid destruction of the forests — primarily by industrial and agricultural development in Third World nations — is paving the way for accelerated global warming and could jeopardize countless species of plant and animals, according to the Rainforest Action Network. Since World War II, about half of the world's rain forests have been lost, the group said.

In addition to raising funds and awareness of th—
Spataro hopes to make it into th—
Record—

Man rides range for rain forests in attempt to increase awareness

By AMY BOARDMAN
Globe-News Staff Writer

Amarillo is the latest stopping point for a Tucson, Ariz., horseman riding across the continent to increase awareness of the earth's rain forests.

Lucian Spataro, 31, his 8-year-old Arabian gelding Sweet William and his four-person, three-RV support team began their trek on May 19 at the shore of the Pacific Ocean in Los Angeles. They plan to end in September in New York, about 3,000 miles away.

The increasingly rapid destruction of the forests — primarily by industrial and agricultural development in Third World nations — is paving the way for accelerated global warming and could jeopardize countless species of plant and animals, according to the San Francisco-based Rainforest Action Network. Since World War II, about half of the world's rain forests have been lost, the group said.

"It's the ecosystem we're losing the quickest," Spataro said of the forests that cover about 2 percent of the earth's surface. "If you don't have an environment, who cares about the rest? It's the basis of everything we do. AIDS and homelessness cease to be a problem if you have no ecosystem."

Along the 1,500 mile route they have covered so far, Spataro and company have attend-

ed fund-raisers and talked to just about anyon— within shouting distance about rain forests.

"It adds up," he said. They probabl— reach about 50 people a day just by ridin— through small towns and at the trailer park— they stop at every night, he said.

By the time they reach New York, Spatar— estimates he will have talked to several thou— sand people about the forests.

"It's a real grass-roots approach to gener— ate interest, but it's probably the best way," — he said.

In addition to raising funds and awareness— of the issue, Spataro hopes to make it into th— Guinness Book of World Records for one— man, one-horse cross-country riding.

The board of directors for the ride is in the— process of organizing a 200-horse march into— Washington, D.C., once the team reaches tha— point. By the end of the ride, the group hope— to have raised close to $1 million for rain for— est projects, such as teaching residents mor— prudent ways to cultivate the land withou— jeopardizing the forests.

The team is staying at the Overnite Traile— Inn east of town until Sunday.

"Some people think we're a bit eccen— tric," he said. "It's going to take some eccen— tricities to make people aware of this issu— quick enough. We just want Congress and th— president to realize that there are people con— cerned about the issue."

Henry Bargas / Globe-News

Lucian Spataro and his horse Sweet William crusade for the preservation of the earth's rain forests.

OKLAHOMA

CHAPTER SIX:
THE CALM BEFORE THE STORM

ABOVE and OPPOSITE Mayor Floyd Craig presents March Along and Lucian with a check from the City of Cordell in front of the Washita County Courthouse.

BELOW Main Street, Cordell Oklahoma. Cordell rolled out the red carpet for the Ride Across America team with a place to stay free of charge and a real small town welcome wherever we went.

I call Oklahoma "the calm before the storm" because some of our toughest times were yet to come. We had ridden through the Texas panhandle on Interstate 40. We were planning to cut through Oklahoma in a straight line on secondary roads, then north again along Old Route 66 into Joplin, Missouri. We were halfway across now.

On August 9th, we rode into Cordell, Oklahoma, a town of about 5,000 residents, and probably had our most enjoyable stay yet. Cordell's mayor, Floyd Craig, met us at the courthouse, the focal point of the town square, and presented us with a check from the City of Cordell. He also offered to let us stay at the city park for free for as long as we wanted.

We had people from Cordell stop in all day long and each evening to wish us well and to talk about grain and hay prices, and the economy, and were well-informed about the rainforest.

Cimarron
River

TULSA

OKLAHOMA CITY

OPPOSITE Joyce Braden kept an eye on the horses and handled the horse chores while Brad and Lucian tended to the ride and ride logistics.

We shared the limelight that week with a groundbreaking ceremony for Cordell's newest industry, a chicken-processing plant. A Cordell resident had been in the East at a party with friends when the host mentioned he was looking for a new site in the Midwest to process chicken. The resident had promoted Cordell as a great location, and one desperately in need of new business. After two years of lobbying, Cordell now had a chicken-processing plant that would employ about 150 workers. We were invited to the groundbreaking ceremony as guests of the city of Cordell.

I rode early that morning, about 3:00 a.m., so I could attend the groundbreaking. All of the city and state officials were there. As Mayor Craig introduced them, they each made a brief comment. Then, the city presented the Cordell resident who made it all happen with an official "Thank You."

I wanted to see firsthand how this plant operated. I love chicken and have been known to sit and eat 20-plus thighs at one sitting. On the road, I would often eat 15 or more pieces of chicken at one meal. Brad used to say that I ate like an Indian. I wouldn't eat for days and then I could consume a whole buffalo, or in this case, a cargo of chickens.

My real interest, however, wasn't in the food, but in the facility. I'd been in and out of a lot of manufacturing plants, and I wanted to see how technically modern this facility would be, and whether they used robots or automated equipment. I was impressed—this was a fully automated facility. They could process and package several thousand chickens per hour. Most of the 150 people employed by the plant were administrative or shipping personnel. It wasn't as I had envisioned it at all. People came in contact with chicken parts only twice, at the onset and at the end of the process.

At the end of the tour, everyone reassembled in the lobby and had an opportunity to do a taste test. After going through the plant, my appetite plummeted and I did not eat my usual 15-plus pieces. The tour did not seem to affect the appetites of the others as much, and everyone dove in. Just as Bob, Bea and I were getting ready to leave, Mayor Craig mentioned to the crowd that Cordell was also proud to be hosting another group of celebrities, the Ride Across America team, and asked us to speak.

I spoke briefly about the ride and the rainforest, but for some strange and unusual reason I felt uncomfortable speaking about the rainforest in a chicken-processing plant. Maybe it was bad karma from the thousands of chickens that had gone through there!

We had a choice to make in Cordell: we could stop and rest up a week or two, or bring in a third horse. Our dilemma was two-fold: I was trying to finish the ride in six months or

less, so we needed to average just over 20 miles per day, every day. We also needed to stay on a relatively tight schedule to attend the various fund-raisers, speaking engagements, and publicity events that RAN had set up along the route. In addition, I didn't want to finish the ride in a snowstorm on the East Coast. Our schedule was very important, and we needed to maintain our 20-mile average each day. The pace was tough on everybody but mostly on the horses, and they were always our first obligation.

At this point in the ride, we had about 1,600 miles under our collective saddle. Of those, 1,400 were on Sweet William and the balance on March Along. To keep up the pace, Mrs. Tankersley, Dr. Hancock, and Brad decided to bring in another Arabian horse to work in tandem with March Along as we moved toward the East Coast. So Mrs. Tankersley sent an Al-Marah trailer out from Tucson with a driver and a fresh horse. Sweet William would be sent back to rest.

The driver, John Winnicki, drove all night and all day and got into Cordell, Oklahoma with Sea Ruler on August 10th. The last time I had seen John was back in Flagstaff, so his encouragement was well-received. The last time I had seen Sea Ruler was three months earlier.

Sea Ruler was a six-year-old endurance horse. He had competed in several endurance events before the ride. During our training in Tucson, I worked all three horses all the way up to the day we left for the West Coast to begin the event.

Al-Marah had made the decision to use Sweet William as the lead-off horse just two weeks before the start of the event, and we'd intended to take Sweet William as far as possible, and hopefully, all the way.

Back in Tucson three months before, Sea Ruler had personally been my first choice as lead-off horse. He was a bit flighty, though, and much younger and less mature than either Willy or March Along. Before I began working Sea Ruler, his previous rider told me that he would shy at almost anything—stationary or moving—and sometimes even at his own shadow. However, when I worked with Ruler in Tucson on the city streets and trails, not once did he shy.

I had been a little disappointed when Al-Marah chose Sweet William over Ruler, but I was learning quickly that in the horse business, like in sports, the athlete does what the coach says and that works best. It becomes a problem when the athlete tries to play coach or questions the coach; then, things can fall apart.

Al-Marah was the coach and trainer, and I was the rider. This ride was no different than, say, for example, the Kentucky Derby: the jockey rides and the trainer tells the jockey how to take the horse out that day, slow or fast, and how far to take him. The jockey's job is to listen to the horse and communicate this to the trainer and to keep on riding.

With this in mind, when I got back from a day of riding, Brad and I would discuss any problems I might have had with the horse or with the route, and Brad would make some mental notes or scribble something in his notepad. Each day we would make necessary adjustments.

After each days ride, Brad and Lucian would wash the horses with warm water and rub their backs with a salt water solution to toughen their hide. Joyce would then comb and brush them down and braid their tails so they were ready for the next day's ride.

The rider's feedback is essential in the decision-making process. As the rider, I had the best feel for how a horse was moving that day—if he was ready to move out or was lagging, how his gait was, whether he was tight or loose, and his attitude, which was probably the most important factor. Like people in such an event, a horse will develop an attitude either as a result of his being tired or bored or off his feed—you name it.

AM Sweet William, as the lead-off horse, did it all. He was an eight-year-old grey gelding who, before this trip, had been considered an accomplished Hunter Jumper, winning several awards and events. He was also a quiet horse, steady through rain, heat, mountains, water and a hundred small towns and cities. He did not have the emotional surges in energy that Sea Ruler had or the stoic outlook that March had; his attitude was steady and relentlessly persevering.

I described his demeanor as "He Went After It...." He was slow and steady, ears pricked forward, just clopping along as I ticked off the miles: 30 miles to Riverside, 400 to Arizona, 800 to New Mexico, 1,200 to Texas, 1,600 to Oklahoma.

AM Sea Ruler, in contrast, was a taller, leaner, almost gangly-looking Arab standing next to Willy, who had the perfect, typical Arab physique. Sea Ruler was like a little kid—he was very playful and tried often to get March Along upset or bothered, just for fun. He had a tremendous amount of energy and was always ready to pick up the pace, even on that last mile at the end of a 20-mile day.

AM March Along was a twelve-year-old gray gelding, a ranch horse for seven years. He was the oldest horse of the three, and I rode him in situations where I needed a dependable, steady mount, usually through city streets and through small towns. I had begun our training in Tucson with March Along and then began working Sea Ruler and finally, Sweet William. March, as Joyce would call him, had a more philosophical, unruffled attitude. So did Sweet William. Unlike those two, Sea Ruler could turn on a dime and would often catch me napping.

I think Sweet William knew better than we did that he had a job to do. To this day, I feel that in his own way, he knew what it would take to get it done. I know he was just as disappointed as I was when John Winnicki loaded him up and pulled away, leaving us all standing there close to tears. The pact that William and I had made back in California was still intact, but now everything was different. All these horses knew one another and had been raised together at Al-Marah. I had trained all three of them back in Tucson.

Now, as Willy pulled out of the park, he sent a high shrill whinny to the other two horses as if to say, "Stay the course, I'm passing the torch to you. Take care of this team, because I'll be watching from Tucson." This was only the second time I'd heard him whinny, the first being a more comical response to the preacher in Gallup.

In unison, both Sea Ruler and March Along whinnied back as if to say, "I've got your back." It was truly an emotional moment and sent a tingle up my spine. Once again I sensed the bond between these horses and myself, and I had a sense, as I had back in California, that we would make it...together.

After Sweet William went back to Tucson for a much-needed rest, we began to alternate Sea Ruler and March Along every other day and sometimes even on the same day. I was now averaging about 27 miles per day with 1,300 miles left to go.

Alternating the horses as we rode toward the East Coast allowed me to ride every day with no days off for rest. We had previously been resting Sweet William every five or six days. At that pace, we would finish in six months, which would be November. I wanted to finish in less than six months. With both horses, we were now averaging about 210 miles every seven days and some days rode 45 miles or more.

Now the question was: *Could I keep up the pace?* I was beginning to have problems with my knees and my back in addition to our riding, I was exercising other muscles by running five miles each day to counterbalance the strain of riding. This helped, but my knees were beginning to feel the strain.

I also had a hard time keeping my weight up; I was now about 143 pounds, down, from a pre-ride weight of about 165. As a result, I had no rear end and was bruising my butt bones. This was very painful, and I often rode out of the saddle, standing in the stirrups or flexing my inner thigh to ride lighter in the saddle. I would often ask Brad if I was sitting properly and if he thought there were any adjustments I could make to relieve the pain. I just couldn't understand how it could be so painful. There were no adjustments I could make—I simply did not have enough butt muscle or fat for padding. After coming to this conclusion, I slowed my running to every other day so that I could put some weight back on. As a wrestler in high school, I remember dropping 20 pounds every week to make weight at 126 pounds. The result: I was not able to sit for long periods of time in a hard chair.

Along the Oklahoma stretch, we did a lot of night riding. The horses and I liked the cool breezes and light traffic. It was tough on the support crew, though. We were bound and determined to ride every step of the way, and to do this, we had to get around many man-made obstacles when traffic was minimal. It was easier when we were night riding.

At the end of each day's ride, we would note our stopping point with a marker, or circle the mile marker on the map. Finding those markers or that location in the dark the next morning was often a very frustrating experience. I can remember, on several occasions, we drove or walked for hours up and down a particular stretch of road looking for a marker.

We avoided riding at night on Friday and Saturday because here in the United States in 1989, one out of three drivers on the road those evenings was impaired. A white horse and rider quickly appearing in the dark on the road, as if from nowhere—well, it's enough of a shock for a sober driver, let alone for someone who has had a few drinks.

Bridges were another obstacle we had to contend with, plan for and scout in advance. On the Interstate, the bridges have very little leeway, maybe five feet from the lane to the rail, sometimes less. Thus far on the ride, we had crossed dozens of these bridges, and our approach to the bridge on the North Fork of the Red River was fairly typical.

OPPOSITE Storm clouds brewing over wild flowers in Oklahoma. The calm before the storm – both on the ride and from an environmental standpoint, as we now have ecological consequences brewing just over the horizon.

As we rode up to the bridge, it looked no different from the many interstate bridges we had crossed thus far. It was a little longer, and that always concerned me because it meant that trucks and cars were going by at high speeds within two or three feet of us for a longer period.

Because we were riding with traffic, these vehicles would come up behind us very quickly and very close. There wasn't much room for error or for indecision. It was very hard to maneuver or to turn around if need be, so once we were on the bridge, our best bet was to keep moving forward. The sun was just coming up, and it was still a little dark out. We had become very accustomed to these interstate bridges.

All of these factors, in combination with my preoccupation with the upcoming rest stop, caused me to ride into a very dangerous situation without thinking. About one-half of the way across the bridge, we encountered a row of orange road markers in the leeway between the rail and the right lane. This automatically cut our five feet of clearance to about three feet, forcing us to skirt the markers and to ride closer to traffic.

At this same point on the bridge, the middle two lanes were being repaired. All the traffic on the bridge was being funneled through the far oncoming lane and the lane adjacent to us. Usually drivers would move over to the far lane when they saw us on a bridge, but in this case, they could not do that.

To add to the situation, the repair team started jack-hammering on the bridge, sending vibrations throughout the whole structure. Sea Ruler did not like this. Now, add one more variable to this muddle: a string of semi trucks, ten of them spaced 150 feet apart, going at least 80 miles per hour. These trucks were no more than 18 inches from us as we threaded the needle between the markers and the lane on this vibrating and pinging bridge. If I stuck my left hand straight out, I would have been able to touch the trucks. Stopping would have made Sea Ruler even more nervous, so we kept going.

It took the trucks about five minutes to get by. At that point, we were about two-thirds of the way across the bridge. Usually horses can handle frightening stimuli if they come in slowly and one at a time. In this case, the stimulation was coming from all directions at once, through Ruler's hooves in the form of vibrations from the jack-hammering, the trucks 18 inches away, and from the unfamiliar orange markers that were teetering from the wind from the trucks. Had one of those markers fallen over and rolled around, Ruler might have immediately shied, possibly into our safety margin of 12 to 18 inches, and right into the active traffic lane—a potential disaster.

We crossed the bridge without further incident. After that very close call, I was sure to scout all bridges and took nothing for granted. I had begun the trip in this cautious manner, taking nothing for granted and scouting everything. At this point we were just getting a little lazy and too comfortable. What we previously considered dangerous we now accepted as routine, but deep down I knew that complacency was something that we had to avoid whenever possible.

Later, when we started crossing more and more rivers, the construction of each bridge became of primary importance. Many bridges did not have concrete surfaces to ride across on, but were made of perforated steel so that water could drain through. This also allowed both me and the horse to see the river below. To add to the problem, these bridges also made a pinging noise when we were crossing on horseback and a roar or rumble as trucks and cars would pass.

On some of the smaller bridges, there was a sidewalk with a rail. The problem with these bridges was that the rail was only slightly higher than the knee of the horse. If for some reason the horse shied toward this rail, it would be very easy at the dizzying height for him to panic and to bump up against the rail.

Our procedure in most cases was to scout the bridge the day before and see if we could cross it without an escort. We observed the traffic patterns and asked about rush-hour times or whether traffic on the bridge was more congested on some days. We also asked about the construction of the bridge: Did it have a sidewalk or a berm that we could ride on?

If we determined that I could do it without an escort, Brad would head on back to camp. If not, we would agree on a time and a place based on the conditions that day and the topography. Then we would meet just this side of the bridge at a given time.

I found out that late at night and early in the morning, before traffic started at about 4:30 a.m.–5:00 a.m., were the best times to cross most bridges. Brad would meet us and lead us across the bridge. He would be traveling about 10 miles an hour, and I would trot with the horse's nose up against the back of the truck or the trailer, as close to the right side as possible.

This I did for two reasons: first, so that Brad could see us in his right mirror out of the blind spot, and second, so that we were as far away as we could be from oncoming traffic. Vehicles coming up from behind would often be backed up for a mile when we were crossing some of the longer bridges.

From the river below, it would have made an interesting picture to see a trailer with a horse and rider trotting right behind, and then right behind them a string of cars backed up for often a mile or more.

On another occasion, on this same stretch of Interstate, I rode down through a small stream to avoid a bridge. This time I was riding March Along. After crossing the stream I found, much to my dismay, that we were now entangled in thick mesh netting used by the highway department to keep grass seed and foliage in place along the highway.

March Along had "Easyboots" on, and the clips on these boots got caught in the mesh. If horses can't move their feet, they have a tendency to panic, especially on the side of a steep embankment. I didn't want March Along to get tangled in the mesh, panic, and roll down the hill, so I coaxed him up the hill, stopping every step to cut the netting off the clips. This unscheduled delay took about an hour, while Brad was patiently waiting at our water stop, which was about a two-hour ride up the road.

Because Brad and Joyce were well known Arabian trainers and ranch managers, having them with us was a big advantage as we hit the Midwest and later the East Coast. Bob and Bea were handling logistics, on-the-road media and fund-raising, as well as filming the ride.

I was pleased to see that Bob, Bea, Brad and Joyce really got along well together. It was like a family of sorts—we had our good days and our bad days, but regardless, we always got together at the end of the day for a Happy Hour. Bea and Joyce would bring out appetizers before dinner, usually cheese and crackers and often, if we were taking the next day off, a beer or two, and we would sit around and talk about the events of that day or our activities for the next day. This was usually early in the evening, about 7:00 p.m. I would be in bed within an hour or two. Brad and Bob and Bea and Joyce would stay up late talking and sharing stories.

If we were taking the following day off, I'd stay up, too, and we would all sit around after dinner and talk about the area we were in and the people we met—always the people. For example, there was Mr. Baskins, the blacksmith….

One day I saw Brad off in the distance, standing next to the rig talking with a man. As I rode up, Brad introduced me to Harry Baskins, a nationally known farrier (blacksmith). Baskins had seen Brad parked on the edge of the highway and had stopped to inquire if he needed any help. One thing led to another, and both Brad and I got a lesson on the iron anvil.

We learned that an iron anvil is not just a hunk of metal against which a blacksmith pounds horse shoes to shape them. It's a tool for the blacksmith, just as a paint brush is a tool for a painter. With an anvil, a blacksmith can shape a shoe to fit any horse, depending on the design of the anvil, the type of material and the way the iron cures.

The "ping" or ring that an anvil makes when a blacksmith strikes it will tell you if you are working with a responsive or a dead anvil. Baskins told us that when you walk into a horse show, you can always tell by the ping of the anvil which blacksmith will be doing the most business. The best blacksmiths' anvils practically sing.

Bea, Joyce, and I each kept a daily journal. Sometimes we perceived incidents in the same manner, but often we saw events quite differently, as shown in our journals.

For example, both Joyce and Bea wrote about our stay at Fort Cobb State Park near a small town called Albert, Oklahoma. I was numb at this point and made no reference in my journal about our stay at that park. We had been riding along Highway 152 toward Oklahoma City and passed through the town of Corn, a Mennonite community of about 1,100 people. I was in the saddle, so the rest of the team stopped in Corn to eat breakfast. Bea mentioned in her journal that they had enjoyed "Veronikas," pancakes rolled around dry cottage cheese mixed with egg and dipped in gravy. Joyce had steak and eggs.

Bea went on to write later that day that we were camped now below the Fort Cobb State Park Dam. (This would not be the last time we camped below a dam.) Bill and Kathy Orel owned that land and leased it to the state park, where employees had cleared a portion of it for a vegetable garden, two port-o-johns, grills, a fireplace and picnic tables. They also

An Amish buggy in Missouri. The Amish lead a very environmentally gentle lifestyle and are known for simple living, plain dress and a reluctance to adopt many of the conveniences of modern technology. The largest concentration of Amish west of the Mississippi River is in Missouri.

had several horses in a field adjacent to the park, and these new horses kept Ruler and March company. One of them was a pregnant mare, and she got so excited when she saw March and Ruler that she slipped and fell, rolling down the hill. Luckily, she was only three months pregnant and was not injured.

The Orels allowed us to use the facility at no charge as the State of Oklahoma's contribution to the rainforest campaign. That evening, we went out for dinner at the Grubstake in Albert, which was owned by Bill Orel's cousin.

After dinner, I wanted to play some pool, so we all crossed the street and walked into the only open bar we could find. It was a tavern with a juke box and three pool tables. It was Ladies' Night—our kind of place. We were determined that we would keep this night very friendly with the locals, as we were still recovering from our earlier altercation. We were a bit gun shy of any new hiccups with the locals, especially when you combine night riding into small towns with drivers on the road who may have been drinking.

The team – Lucian, Bea, Joyce, Brad, and Bob – are relaxing by the fire at the end of the day after a "Long Ride," horse chores and maybe even a media event.

Brad and Joyce danced while Bea and Bob and I watched the pool tables to determine who might easily be beaten. There were no sure bets—they were all really good. As Bob sized the place up, I tried to put quarters down on one table. There were too many quarters up and they all belonged to one man, who had essentially tied the table up while he was winning. If he lost, he had quarters down to keep on playing as well. The table was clearly his.

Noticing our frustration, the female bartender came over to talk with Bob. She explained the rules, which we already knew, but we thought of adding a new twist. We offered to buy the guy a beer so we could use the table. Brad and I started playing, and soon we were both on a roll, playing way over our heads and putting everything in. It was getting to be an impressive show, and one that attracted some attention.

Johnny, the player who held the table before us, came over and began talking with Bob. He told us, "Guys from Oklahoma don't have much else to do except work and play pool: that's why we're so good."

This guy had his own cue, so I should have known better, but Bob and Brad managed to convince Joyce and Bea to play Johnny for control of the table. Johnny could not believe he was going to play two women. About halfway through the game, the Ride Across America team got some lucky breaks and dropped five balls. Now they were even with Johnny. Once, when it was Joyce's shot, Johnny went to the men's room and Brad saw his chance—he dropped four of our balls in different pockets. Johnny came out and wouldn't believe Joyce had shot them in.

And yes, he accused us of cheating. Our team started to get a bit nervous and Brad started to tease Johnny, gently at first, as only cowboys can. It worked and Johnny loosened up a bit. But he made sure, by clearing the table, that the team knew that he was the best player in Albert.

Bob and Bea were subtle pranksters. Brad told jokes and had a very large repertoire for any audience and Joyce was great with the kids we met along the way. She was also our "people person"—she talked with everybody who stopped to visit the camp for as long as they wanted to talk.

However, Bea was deathly afraid of bugs and spiders. Joyce, too, would often comment on the bugs we'd run into. I saw all this as an opportunity to frighten Bea, and one day late on my ride, I saw a snake on the side of the road. Further inspection showed that it was only a snakeskin, a perfect prop for a prank I wanted to play on Bea.

Snakeskin has a very peculiar feel to it, and just by looking at it you know how it would feel to touch it. I was not a stranger to the sensation because as a youngster I'd had snakes for pets. When I returned to camp, I made a point of visiting the Winnebago and when no one was around, quietly dropped the snakeskin right next to the Kachina dolls.

BELOW Historically, snakes have been an object of dread and fascination and they both repel and fascinate the human mind. The reaction we humans have when we feel a snake up against our skin is a primal survival instinct and without having the experience you can only imagine how you would react when waking up from a sound sleep to find a snake curled up next to you in bed.

OPPOSITE Headlights from our vehicles, as a beautiful sun sets on our campground in Oklahoma.

Several days went by and I questioned Brad and Joyce, who were in on the prank, to see if they had seen any particular reaction. So far, no reaction, and even two days later, there was still no reaction. We had no days off at this point, so I was usually exhausted when I hit the sack.

It never took more than a minute to fall asleep, but one evening was to be a little different than most. I was tossing and turning to get comfortable when my leg rubbed up against something very rough and dense. I quickly woke up, terrified to realize that I had a snake in my bed! The snake wasn't moving yet, so I told myself, *Okay, now just be calm. Wake up slowly, think before you react and don't make any quick moves.* As I began to become more conscious, I tried to come up with a plan to overcome this snake.

I knew that a bright light might confuse the snake long enough for me to roll off the bed. Chanting "One, two, three," I flicked on the lights, threw off the covers and rolled out of the bed.

There lay the snakeskin. I breathed a sigh of relief, then chuckled as I realized I'd been "pranked." However, I was not going to give my team members the satisfaction of knowing how shocked I'd been to wake up in bed with a snake.

For the next month, the same snakeskin passed back and forth between all three vehicles and no one said a word to anyone or expressed shock on finding it wherever it appeared: in the blender, in the bed, under the pillow, in shoes....

I think Bob and Bea ended up with the skin and drove all the way to Connecticut before they found it with them.

Riding on toward Oklahoma City, we passed a town called Nowhere, Oklahoma. Now, I must tell you about Nowhere. It's perfectly named because it's the hardest place to find, bar none. You never actually arrive in Nowhere because once you get there, you are not just in Nowhere. You really are NOWHERE!

We rode through Oklahoma City in a deluge of rain—in fact, seven straight days of rain. The ground was so soft that March Along stretched a tendon and pulled up lame. Brad had him rest for fifteen days and I rode Sea Ruler for the next two weeks straight, still averaging over 21 miles per day and often 26 and 27 miles.

We were now beginning to encounter many rivers and streams—it was a very tough stretch. I crossed the Canadian River in Oklahoma in the early morning, having begun that ride at midnight. We also crossed the Arkansas River in the early morning.

We had now been on the road for several months with no R & R. We just couldn't afford any time off, as we wanted to maintain the pace, and we had scheduled events to attend. My insistence that we maintain the pace was grinding on myself and the team. For this reason, Oklahoma was a stretch of extremes—giant swings in mood from total elation, pranks and good times, to total depression.

The sadness at replacing Willy, the ongoing accelerated tempo, the routines and the rhythms, the midnight rides and scouting expeditions ... we found ourselves on automatic pilot as one day blended into the next.

OPPOSITE Residents of Tulsa could relate to our message as this is considered "Green Country" with heavily wooded rolling hills, mountain lakes, and streams, as opposed to western and central Oklahoma which are geologically similar to the rest of the Great Plains. Average precipitation totals around Tulsa are about 40 inches per year, making it considerably wetter and greener than the rest of the state.

Equestrian Crossing U.S. to Educate Americans to Rain Forest Woes

By Lisa Tresch
World Staff Writer

Lucian Spataro is riding horseback across the country to warn people that the world's rain forests are in trouble.

During a stop in Tulsa Thursday, Spataro, who is a member of the Rainforest Action Network (RAN), said Oklahoma is a challenging place to educate people about rain forests.

"People don't realize that just because there are no rain forests in this part of the country, doesn't mean they aren't affected by the deterioration of the forests."

Spataro began his 2,800-mile "Ride Across America" in Los Angeles on May 19 and will finish the record-breaking ride in Maryland in September. He will travel through about 13 states at a rate of about 22 miles a day.

He hopes to establish a Guinness World Record for horse riding distance and time during the journey. He also hopes to let people know the realities involved in destroying the rain forests.

"The forests are destroyed at a rate of one acre per second," Spataro said. "If the rate stays steady, by the year 2000 there will be virtually no rain forests. They used to cover 14 percent of the earth's surface, and in 35 years, we've reduced that to 7 percent."

Spataro said the rain forests are a moderator of weather, and often make the difference of how much rain is received and how much humidity exists.

"As we ride into some of the smaller towns, we find that people are not really aware of the rain forest problems," Spataro said. "We really are concentrating on raising the awareness level about the issue."

Spataro has traveled on Interstate-40 through California, Arizona, New Mexico, Texas and Oklahoma.

Fund-raisers held along the way have provided RAM with almost $80,000. The money, he said, will go toward educational programs, printed materials and lobbying efforts.

"This is not really an activist thing," Spataro said. "It's very low-key. We just want to let people know what is going on and tell them the realities of the problems."

Spataro, 31, is an equestrian trainer from Tucson, Ariz., who came up with the idea for the cross-country ride about two years ago. Planning, he said, has taken two years.

"Our goal was to raise $1 million," he said. "I don't think we really expected to do that, but it is something to shoot for."

Spataro is alternating riding several horses, and traveling with eight other people who follow him in recreational vehicles. The group stayed at the Hilltop RV Park in Sapulpa Thursday night.

The Al-Marah Ranch of Tucson, Ariz., provided Spataro with Arabian horses and corporate sponsors are providing tack and gear.

RAN is a non-profit corporation based in San Francisco

World staff photo by Ron Hart

Lucian Spataro puts a bridle on Sea Ruler.

MISSOURI AND ILLINOIS

CHAPTER SEVEN:
WE HIT THE WALL

ABOVE Which is worse? The pain is unbearable but my "Breakfast of Champions" makes it all go away.

BELOW Headed into Joplin, Missouri.

OPPOSITE Lucian and Sea Ruler taking a break on the side of the road in Missouri.

If Oklahoma had been the calm before the storm, we'd probably started our sprint to the finish about 700 miles too soon. Our elation was premature because somewhere between Tulsa, Oklahoma, and Joplin, Missouri, I "hit the wall"—that point in a race when you ask yourself, "What the heck am I doing out here?"

We were riding in 100 degree heat, and the humidity was so thick you could cut the air with a knife. This combination—wet heat and fatigue, mosquitoes, ticks, flies and gnats—began to do a real tap dance on my head. We were all getting more than a little road-weary. I was living on Tylenol mixed in with pineapple for breakfast along with my normal milk and cereal. This concoction helped eased the pain in my knees and my butt bones. I was now twenty five pounds lighter than at the start of the ride.

We had all been on the road now for more than three months. The close quarters and long hours were wearing on the humans but the horses were getting stronger and we were now averaging a little over 26 miles per day.

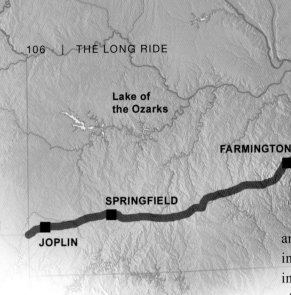

Lake of
the Ozarks

FARMINGTON

SPRINGFIELD

JOPLIN

OPPOSITE It is hard to believe, but to put this in perspective for you, every second of every day, one and one-half acres of rainforest are lost with tragic consequences. In the time it has taken us to travel the distance we've traveled in Missouri alone, we've lost an area of rainforest that is in fact the size of the state of Missouri.

But the honeymoon was over. The adrenaline we had produced at the start was gone, and we had just begun to realize how far we had yet to go. On August 23rd, 1989, we crossed into Missouri at a point just east of Joplin. This is the center of a four-state region that includes Oklahoma. Missouri, Arkansas, and Kansas, and was a little more than two-thirds of the way across the country via our route. As I was crossing the border into Missouri out of Oklahoma, the Joplin newspaper caught us. The pictures taken by the reporters of us standing in the rain on the side of the road revealed how badly we were hurting. Just looking at those photos, I could understand why our morale was so low.

Intermingled with the pain, as always, was the saving grace of some very humorous moments. Two funny things happened while we were in Joplin. The first was a fluke. I was, at this point, a little tired of repeating to people the same old story about my ride and the rainforest. The response was always an incredulous, "Are you serious?"

When I told them I was riding to New York from Los Angeles, people would often want to talk, and that talking time really added up. Now we could no longer afford the delay, and the farther east we rode, the harder it was to complete a day's ride. Everyone wanted to stop and talk. Although we knew that we had to talk about the rainforest at every opportunity, by this time it was becoming very tiring. I was always torn between stopping and talking and trying at the same time to maintain this record-breaking pace. Because we had timed our events to coincide with this pace, we were further pressed to push on and keep up the pace.

With all of this in mind, toward the end of some days I would catch myself saying to people who would ask where I was going, "I'm just riding to the next town. By the way, how far is that?" Or sometimes, I would almost automatically hand out a brochure and a brief explanation, and keep on riding. This usually worked, but one time I was stopped.

We had arrived in Joplin the day before a big article in the local paper featured our ride. It was also on the news. I wanted to purchase some clothes and needed to get some pants altered at the Polo store in Joplin because I had lost so much weight that my pants no longer fit and I needed them for the coming fund-raiser in St. Louis.

At the store, the clerk said, "Fine. Come back in two days and we'll have them ready for you." As we were making small talk, the clerk asked if I was in town on business or pleasure. I responded, "Neither." He looked at me as if to say, "What else is there?" I gave no further explanation; I was so tired and sweaty from the ride and I had literally no energy that day.

People

Friday,
August 25, 1989

The Joplin Globe

Globe Photos/VINCE ROSATI

Lucian Spataro, 32, will be traveling through Missouri today on his cross-country ride to call attention to endangered rain forests.

Lucian Spataro and his Arabian horse travel about 25 miles day.

Rider hitches up to ecological issue

By Marti Attoun
Globe Staff Writer

Lucian Spataro and Sweet William, his Arabian gelding, were happy to trot into Oklahoma, but were even happier to hit Missouri. It means their 3,000-mile trek is more than half finished.

Spataro, 32, an environmentalist and athlete from Tucson, Ariz., is riding across America to raise public awareness and funds for the Rainforest Action Network. He left Los Angeles, Calif., on May 19 and hopes to reach Washington D.C. in early October.

Bob Shepard, who is videotaping the ride and helping with publicity, says the ride's purpose is twofold: to draw attention to the country's depleting tropical rain forests so the public will talk to people who have impact on policies affecting the rain forests, and to raise $1 million in contributions.

Spataro rides about 25 miles a day and makes frequent stops along the way to address civic groups, distribute brochures and attend fund-raisers.

Rain forests cover less than two percent of the globe, but are home to as many as 5 million species of plants, animals and insects. More than 25 percent of all medicines marketed in U.S. pharmacies come from plants grown in rain forests. More than half of the original rain forests have been destroyed.

Spataro also hopes to set a Guinness World Record for horse-riding distance and time. He's already in the Guinness book for pedaling a tricycle on the bottom of a swimming pool, along with other scuba divers, for 60 hours and 64.96 miles. That effort raised $30,000 for a Tucson charity for battered children.

The Rainforest Action Network, based in San Francisco, Calif., is a non-profit international conservation group. The group achieved a recent victory in preserving the last 28,000 acres of rain forest in Puerto Rico. The group is campaigning now to halt the use of tropical timber imports.

Having had a wake-up that morning at 3:30 a.m. and one scheduled the next day for 4:00 a.m., I was really looking forward to a shower and a nap.

The clerk kept looking at me as if he needed a better answer. So I said, "I'm just passing through town. I'll just be here for a few days because I'm heading east." This seemed to satisfy him and I left.

Little did I know that the coverage the next day would be extensive, with articles on both TV stations, the radio and both papers, front page stuff. Bob Shepard had outdone himself in Joplin—he had the media buzzing about the event.

My return to the store two days later turned out to be pretty amusing. The clerk had alerted the rest of the staff, and they all came out, chanting in unison, "Just heading east, eh?"

"Real slow," they added and, laughing hysterically, they all went back to their jobs.

When the clerk asked me why I hadn't told him what I was doing in town, I replied that I was simply too tired to go through another explanation that day. He answered sympathetically, "Hey, after seeing your interview on TV last night, I can understand that. You still look beat."

I could only respond, "Thanks for the encouragement."

The interview on TV with KOAM in Joplin was interesting. Kevin Petrehn, KOAM's premiere reporter, wanted to do a really unique interview, so he got a horse and rode along beside me. However, Kevin had never been on a horse before and was carrying camera equipment and microphones. The video of that interview, filmed by Bob Shepard, showed Kevin shooting footage and interviewing me as he was riding half on and half off his horse. I was on his left and he was leaning well to his right and the camera equipment was dangling everywhere. His horse was walking sideways as he tried to stay under Kevin. A good horse will do that, and we got a perfect example of this on film. The TV spot came out fine, and we gave Kevin rainforest footage, as well.

Kevin and KOAM did a great job on the spot. It was the best yet, well worth the time and effort we all spent setting it up. CNN used this cut several weeks later on an "Earth Matters" segment, featuring our ride together with a guy who flew an Ultralite plane across Greenland for another environmental cause.

On August 26th, we went up to St. Louis for two fund-raisers. We broke camp that morning and Brad put me on Sea Ruler at 4:30 a.m. I rode 26 miles that day, got off Ruler about 2:30 p.m., and then drove about 450 miles to St. Louis. We took the following day off to attend both events. We then drove back to our stopping point in southern Missouri to continue our ride.

Jim Volz had an evening fund-raiser for us, and earlier that same afternoon we brought Sea Ruler down to the arch in downtown St. Louis for a photo shoot and rainforest rally. We left March Along with a friend of Brad's at our stopping point in southern Missouri. This gave March Along a much needed day of rest, so he was ready to go the day after our fund-raiser. Sea Ruler was a little tired from the trailer ride to St. Louis.

OPPOSITE In a roadside interview with KOAM in Joplin, Lucian stated, "For those people who today still wrongfully assume that the Earth is so immense that humans can't impact the operation of these natural systems, your thinking is just hooey. Our ever increasing human population when combined with new technologies that have dire environmental impacts, have now positioned us to step very hard on these natural systems with dramatic consequences."

Lucian Spataro Sr., Lucian and Luis Lugo celebrating a new business contract, 1987.

Both events went very well and we had more than 150 people attend the fund-raiser at Jim Volz's farm. I got a picture of Brad carrying a "SAVE THE RAINFOREST" picket sign under the arch in St. Louis. I never thought I would see the day that Brad would carry a picket sign in downtown St. Louis. Now, we needed to get him to wear a "SAVE THE RAINFOREST" T-shirt!

These fund-raisers were good for us because they broke up the routine. However, they were very tough on the team and the horses. While we were on the road and riding, we were in a rhythm of sorts, and our routine kept us going. The activities, however, were very tiring because we always had to look our best, act energetic, and appear to be having lots of fun. Given the pace we were trying to maintain daily, that facade was very difficult to sustain. If a child asked us, "Are you having fun?" I always said, "Yes" and smiled and shook hands with everybody.

Yet, all I really wanted to do was crawl into a nice bed and sleep for more than five hours. I knew that the next day, these people would all go home and, sitting comfortably in their easy chairs, read about us in the papers. Meanwhile, we'd be up at 3:00 a.m. riding through some rainstorm in the dark for three hours, and then in the heat of the day for seven more hours.

The fund-raisers were as draining as the riding because I couldn't slack off. We didn't rest before or after the events, and immediately got back on the road.

The strain of riding affected us in other ways. What were previously small differences of opinion in our group now started to increase in size and frequency. I wrote in my journal on August 28th that I almost "lost it," and I found differences building between Brad and myself.

I was pushing very hard and would often ask Brad to double me up with two horses. I was putting in 45 miles a day, back-to-back. This was as tough on me and the team members as it was on the horses, and from Oklahoma on we rode very hard with many 12- and 14-hour days of riding then another five hours of scouting, nonstop.

I was opposed to taking days off, and I made it very clear that we should ride every day, despite inclement weather or difficult terrain. I wanted us to make every effort to work around vehicle problems and ride through weather so we could maintain the pace.

It was August 28, 4:30 a.m. and the rain was beating down in sheets and the wind was buffeting the trailer, making it rattle and shake. I was sitting at the table in the dark, eating out of a can of pineapple and crunching on granola cereal. I had cans and buckets strategically placed around the trailer to catch the water that was dripping in from the leaks in the roof. Everything in my trailer was soaked—clothes, the bed, and the food.

March had just pulled up a bit gimpy going through Oklahoma City, so Ruler was carrying the load and I was still pushing for more mileage. But Brad was concerned; he had heard that there were flash flood warnings and the rain was coming down in waves. Sometimes we couldn't see literally 10 feet in front of us. I was wearing a yellow rain suit that Joyce had bought for Brad and me at a K-Mart. They looked just like those I'd worn as a young child; I even had the matching yellow rain hat. I looked like an older version of Donald Duck!

We had been riding in this weather for four days with one good horse, and I had spoken often by phone with my business partners, Luis Lugo in Mexico and Joe Tooker in Tucson. The news was not good. I played a key role in those businesses and when I left, some important work was not getting done. I felt very guilty about that and tried to help while I was on the road, but to no avail.

To keep riding was a very difficult sacrifice to make because it affected others: we had employees and partners who depended on me. Neither my partners nor I had felt at the time that the marketing and contracting end of the business (which was under my direction) would deteriorate as quickly as it had, and on top of that, we had been caught in an economic downturn.

All of this came crashing down at the same time that we were hitting very bad weather on the ride. Looking back, I can honestly call this point in the ride "the perfect storm" of personal and professional events.

Driving all of this is human population growth and the related demand for food, water, and energy. We humans numbered less than 2 billion at the end of World War II but in the span of less than one generation our population has grown to almost 7 and possibly 9 billion within one generation. This growth and the related consumption is putting enormous pressure on these natural systems worldwide.

On August 28th, 4:30 a.m., Brad strongly vetoed my decision to ride that day. Unfortunately, this was the day after I got the news from my business partners that we were in trouble. I was already upset, and I felt Brad's decision was motivated less by the poor riding conditions and more by a desire for personal comfort. So I let him know how I felt.

I told Brad I thought we should ride and that the weather should not be a factor. We had been riding in the rain very uncomfortably now for four days, and I was prepared to continue, come hell or in this case high water. Brad replied that we were risking injury to both the people and the horses. I retorted that it was no more risky now than on any other day of the week. In the past, I had tried not to overrule Brad, because I trusted his judgment.

I found out later that it was very hard for Brad to defend why he decided to do this or that because often it was a "seat of the pants" or "gut feel" reasoning on his part. With horses, experience can strongly influence one's feelings, which can be difficult to explain to others. When it came to the horse-related issues, even though I disagreed, Brad still had the final say and he could veto the whole day by canceling the ride based on a horse-related issue. This did not happen often and we were usually able to come to some kind of consensus or agreement, but at a price.

The price was that, in this gray area of decision-making, our tensions had begun to build. We often had disagreements over the route I chose to take, while my main concern was the time it would take; comfort and convenience were secondary. Thus, I often chose the straightest, shortest route, which could be difficult for the horses and uncomfortable for the other members of the team and inconvenient to trailer into and out of.

I also wanted to ride every day and go as far as we could, which in some cases was more than Brad felt the horses should do. We were not arguing—we never raised our voices at each other—but we did feel that our mutual support and good-fellowship was ebbing away. At the end of the day, we would go our separate ways and not speak until the next morning.

I am, for the most part, a driven and persistent person, and I demand a lot of myself and the people around me. I have a high energy level and I try to lead by example but I don't often say what I'm thinking. This can be a problem, because the more focused I become, the more quiet I get and this kind of tense confrontation was understandable, considering the strenuous circumstances, close quarters and road fatigue. This was no leisurely stroll across America. We were not only trying to break a record, but also to establish a new, unbeatable record.

I knew we had only one shot at doing this and I wanted us to set a well-documented record that would stand the test of time. I knew that as soon as we set the record and it became public, numerous individuals would be out to break it.

I knew this because in 1982, I had organized a group of scuba divers to set a Guinness Book World Record, and we had actually ridden a bicycle underwater for 64.96 miles in 62 hours! We held that record for the longest underwater bicycle race for less than two years, and as soon as the Guinness Book came out with our record, it was quickly broken.

OPPOSITE Sea Ruler on the left and March Along on the right, always on the lookout for some attention, at our camp in an RV park in Missouri.

I did not want this to happen to our "Ride Across America," and I believed that a single rider and a three-horse ride from coast to coast in five months or less would be unbreakable.

In retrospect, Brad's sense of moderation was a very important component and was essential to our success, not just because it pertained to the horses but also to me and other members of the team. With a moderating force to rely upon, I pushed hard, assuming that he would do his part and say, "Back off," or "Slow down." Without his balance, I doubtless would have done it myself, but I was subconsciously relying on Brad to set my pace. Even though I resented it when he protested, I knew his perspective was important. This push and pull kept us going.

On the same day, I wrote in my journal that I needed to stay in touch with all my old friends and I even listed them. I made a commitment to work harder at my business.

I wrote that I wanted to finish the ride as a "thank you" for the many people who helped us, and that "I feel a growing burden to finish, and that burden comes from all of the well-wishers along the way. We are now riding as much for them as we are for the issue and ourselves."

I ended the journal that day with three comments: The first was something Bazy had told me before we left. She said, "In this kind of event, to finish is to win." Immediately after that I wrote: "Nothing of any real significance was ever accomplished that did not require extreme sacrifice." And finally, I wrote: "If number one and number two are true, then keep it together, whatever it takes."

On that day, it seemed I was little nostalgic, lonesome for home, and close to exhausted. I was on automatic pilot and not very coherent. I cannot remember details from that part of the ride at all—only the start and the finish are vivid, while the middle 1,000 miles are vague—just one long 45-day blur. It was almost like sleep-riding.

On September 1st, things began to take a turn for the better. We had some really good press coverage in Joplin, and just after that I was riding into a little town called Grambia. We were now in Missouri, adjacent to Arkansas. At various points along the way I had been calling in to WJR radio in Detroit to report on our progress and to answer questions about the rainforest, live on the air.

Such events were very difficult to coordinate, and we were typically riding through very unpopulated areas, so finding a phone at the exact time I needed to be on the air was next to impossible. Gas stations, private homes, car phones, a police station, city hall—you name it, we used it. My attempt to find a phone while riding a horse down the road would have been a perfect advertisement for cell phones!

You can imagine some of the conversations I got into trying to convince a local farmer to let me use his private rotary phone to make a long distance call to Detroit, all the while holding onto my white Arabian and talking about saving the rainforest. I asked WJR radio why I couldn't make these calls later in the day after I got off the horse. The problem was that this particular show aired at 10 a.m. and that we were riding west to east. The time difference was one, two or three hours, depending on our location.

I would complete the day's ride between noon and 2:00 p.m. That would mean that I would need to make my phone calls anywhere between 7:00 a.m. and 11:00 a.m., depending on how close we were and whether we were west or east of Detroit. Ordinarily, this would not seem like a difficult task to coordinate, but I was looking for phones on unfamiliar roads, then trying to convince strangers to let me use them. Added to that, I was riding a white horse, dressed more like a runner than a rider, and carrying an MCI calling card.

I got lucky on September 3rd: I had a telephone call set up for 9:15 a.m. Missouri time with WJR. The arrangement was that I had to be on the air, on hold, by 10:10 a.m. their time (9:10 a.m. my time) or they would cancel until the next day.

At 8:55 a.m. I was still two miles outside of the little town of Grambia. I wasn't wearing a watch, but asked a passerby what time it was. So that left me 20 minutes to canter in the last

Bob would spend the morning setting up media interviews for Lucian, who would stop along the way to make these calls. This photograph shows Lucian making a call to a local radio station, with Bob setting up the next call, and March Along taking a break and wondering, "Where are my carrots?"

two miles. I began riding at a very fast trot through the small community, asking people right and left: "Where's the closest phone?"

They all pointed down the road, saying, "At Quik Stop." I arrived in the center of town at the Quik Stop at 9:09 a.m., and I now had one minute to find someone to hold my horse, Sea Ruler, get inside the Quik Stop and make the call from the pay phone just inside the door. People inside the store watched with strange looks on their faces as I walked up to the door and held it open, still hanging onto Ruler. With one hand I reached for the phone, while Ruler stood on the sidewalk.

Luckily, I got through to the program coordinator, Rosanna Kelly, but was immediately put on hold for five minutes until the show began. No one in the store said a word; they just continued to stare. Ruler was now nudging me. He had moved so that he was standing inside the store's door frame, blocking the door so no one could enter or leave the store.

I now had five minutes to organize this potential fiasco so I could finish the pending talk show. I already had everyone's attention so, seeing no other alternative, I broke the silence by announcing to everyone: "I'm going to be on the air in Detroit on a long-distance call for a talk show. Would someone please hold my horse?"

There was no reaction.

Ruler now had half his front end in the store and was gumming the potato chip rack. I mentioned that I was riding across America on this horse and luckily, someone inside the store recognized us. Immediately, everyone broke into smiles and three customers offered to hold Ruler while I completed my phone call. The owner offered me a bottle of juice and a sandwich "on the house" and then called the local paper to do an interview as well. The coverage we had received the day before and that morning in Joplin had helped them all make the connection.

After the talk show interview, I stayed for a while to talk to the local media and several locals, and then I rode on down the road. Another day on the road, another memorable experience.

That same day, I found out that we were only about 60 miles from Fayetteville, Arkansas, a town I had lived in many years ago. That brought back a lot of memories. I wrote in my journal: "Twenty-six years ago, I lived in this area, and it seems like such a long time ago. If I had known at that time that I would be riding a horse through here 26 years hence to save the rainforest, would that have made any significant difference?"

I added: "In this day and time you predict the future based on present-day criteria, no longer on past history. History is no longer a good indicator of what the future will be."

Changes are constant and exponential. What might previously have been a sound process for making a personal or financial decision may not apply in the present or future. Those who recognize this and can be flexible and adaptable will succeed.

A perfect example, I wrote, was the banking crisis and the Third World debt. Who would have thought back in 1985 that lending money to another country would be a bad idea? Countries don't go broke—individuals do, right? Who would have guessed that loans based

OPPOSITE Sea Ruler and Lucian in Grambia at the Quik Stop. The radio interviews that were usually done using public pay phones, garnered a lot of attention and offered us an opportunity to take a break and talk with the local residents who may have heard about the ride and the issue on the radio or in the paper.

on oil projections in Third World countries, and more recently, on mortgages on residential homes, would be a bad bet? But banks lent money against oil assets and residential homes and proceeded to lose everything.

I also wrote that we did not know years ago that, within 50 years, some aspects of technology would have a devastating impact on our environment. Just knowing that history is not necessarily a predictor of the future, and that future new technology will have the greatest single impact on our lives and this environment, has struck a chord of concern in us. Our future is now officially uncertain, and that's scary.

The implications, both positive and negative, for societies as we think of them today are limitless. This is both scary and exciting, and while riding on a horse on such a long journey, I had a lot of time to think!

I wrote that same day: "Maybe I should think less. This is too deep to fathom. I need to leave all this up to politicians, scientists and philosophers." And then I added, "What a combination! If we do that, we are in deep trouble."

On September 1st, we set up a base camp in Montauk Park in southern Missouri. A state park located at the headwaters of the Current River, Montauk serves as a fish hatchery and fishing park. We camped there for five days, and found Montauk probably one of the most beautiful fishing spots in the United States.

As I was riding into the park, it seemed so very familiar, and then I recalled that, when I was six or seven years old, my family had come here from Arkansas in the summer. The place had not changed at all in those 26 years. I found the rural road system in Missouri was also unchanged and just as frustrating in 1989 as it had been in 1963, when our family had driven through this area.

Now, on this ride, we tried in all cases to stay as close to a straight-line route as we possibly could. This forced us to pore over maps in the Midwest and quiz local farmers on the shortest or straightest possible route from point A to point B.

In the northern Ozarks of southern Missouri, the straightest and shortest path was often two very different routes. The terrain and the riding conditions along the road were of utmost concern in this area. Often in Missouri we were on one- and two-lane rural roads and local trails marked with a letter designation. For example, the roads around Montauk Park were marked as LL, LM, LK and JJ. Roads farther east and south were marked with other letter combinations. Obviously, this could be really confusing!

Once, Brad and I were talking with a local store owner about our route. We needed to get to a point about 45 miles farther east along as straight a route as possible. According to the notes in my journal, the directions went something like this: "Take LL about two miles and get off on 168; it's a fire trail. That will take you to F; at F go east about 6 miles and get on CC or AA, either one will take you to PP. There are several roads that run parallel and perpendicular to AA and CC. Don't take them, they include U, WW, H and JJ. They are all

OPPOSITE We rode hundreds of miles on two lane country roads like this one in Missouri. On a positive note, the traffic was light and typically slower and the drivers were more accustomed to horses, but the tight blind corners and narrow berm on the side of the road provided very little margin for error.

dead ends. Stay on CC or AA until you get to B; when you hit B take it east past M and P to Z; Z east will put you within spitting distance of the Mississippi River. Good Luck."

No kidding! Somewhere in there was a mistake. See if you can find it—eventually, we did! It took us three days to cover 45 miles. Nonetheless, it still saved us about four days, since the more northerly route would have taken seven days.

We made it to the river, and on September 9th we crossed the Mississippi at a city called Chester, in Illinois. I was riding March Along and had left Sea Ruler back at camp to rest for a couple of days.

Two days earlier, on September 7th, we'd had an accident that almost ended the trip. We were riding along PP, a narrow rural road with a very steep drop on both sides; rain was coming down in sheets and we could barely see ten feet in front of us. The road was very slippery, and we were straddling the top of the road and the embankment. There was a small hill in the distance, and coming up behind us was a tractor with a hay wagon hooked on behind it.

The tractor was in the center of the road, and just as we approached the hill, the tractor pulled up next to us. As we began to crest it together, the tractor swerved closer to us to make room for any oncoming traffic that could be on the other side. This pushed Ruler and me right off the edge of the road, causing us to walk awkwardly sideways about 25 percent of the way down the embankment.

And then, it happened. Ruler stepped into a huge drainage ditch, a hole at least six feet deep, and went down. With the rain pelting down, we couldn't see the hole, and as we tumbled down the side of the embankment, I rolled out of the saddle to my right and down the hill. My hope was to relieve whatever pressure I could from Ruler. As I started to roll and slide down the hill, I caught myself and looked to my left just in time to see Ruler rolling down the hill right behind me. He was out of control, as this was a very steep embankment, and he rolled right over me and crunched me.

I continued rolling and sliding down to the bottom of the embankment. Then Ruler was up and shaking himself off, the saddle hanging underneath him. Ruler had grass stains and dirt all over him, and was limping as well. I could not not pull myself back into the saddle because I was concerned that he had injured himself and any additional weight might further the damage.

It felt as if I'd twisted my ankle so badly I couldn't walk. So there we were at the bottom of a very steep embankment. The radio we had with us was broken by the fall, the rain was coming down in buckets and I didn't think we could get back up the steep embankment. The guy driving the tractor didn't even look back as he pushed us off the embankment, so no one knew were at the bottom of this ravine. It was quite a mess.

I hobbled along with Ruler along a fence line as I leaned into the saddle stirrup to hold myself up. The pain in my ankle was excruciating and I worried that it was broken. Sea Ruler was limping along on three legs, and the two of us limped along for about a mile until miraculously, he shook it off.

I, on the other hand, still couldn't walk. I had a long lead rope on the saddle, and as we neared the edge of the road as it meandered down off the hill, I threw a lead rope over his head and then let him walk to the edge of the road. I stayed down off the hill below the road. Ruler stopped at the road and just stood there, as he had no more rope.

I was hoping that a car would see him standing without a rider on the side of the road in the rain and stop to help us. As luck would have it, Brad was driving the back roads looking for us and saw Ruler standing on the side of the road in the rain with the lead rope dangling over the edge of the embankment. He slammed on the brakes and stopped just in time. He found me sitting on the ground down below the embankment, drenched but happy that the injury to both of us was just a strain.

Later, I learned that because we were very late, and because the radio had broken in the fall, we had been out of communication with the team. They had been so worried that they'd gone out searching for us. Thank goodness Brad found us.

I took a short trip to the doctor, who confirmed that I was suffering from a severe strain. He suggested that I not ride anymore for a few weeks, but we all knew that wasn't going to happen. After he put the ankle in a soft cast and fortified me with plenty of Tylenol, I was back in the saddle that next day. Call it lunacy, but at this point, nothing was going to stop this ride.

Sea Ruler listens in while Brad and Lucian have a friendly debate over the trade off between what might be the shorter, straighter, and faster route versus maybe a safer but longer route. "Hey, you should have scouted this." "No, you should have scouted this." And on it goes.

WABASH
River

EAST ST. LOUIS

CARMI

Mississippi
River

WEST
FRANKFORT

OPPOSITE Breakfast and lunch were always Tylenol, corn flakes, pineapple and whatever else you could grab at 4 a.m. in the dark. But dinner was a different story and a real treat when we were in a campground that had cooking facilities.

Brad and I talked about how we could tape my ankle in the stirrup to prevent it from moving for the next few days, and Bea and Joyce were very concerned because they knew that another fall would surely break my leg. This would be particularly dangerous if I couldn't get my feet out of the stirrup or worse, if I were dragged in a runaway situation.

We all agreed that if I simply walked and trotted for the next week or until I got the soft cast off, it would be well worth the risk. It worked, and we kept on going.

Now the team was being extraordinarily careful. The farther we rode, the more meticulous I became, and our planning each evening could take up to several hours. I wanted to confirm every detail, which sometimes meant I'd do it while riding.

Brad spent the greater part of his day driving alternate routes in an attempt to determine the straightest, shortest, and safest possible path. Planning inevitably involved a trade-off among three variables: 1) dangerous, narrow rural roads and embankments versus Interstate and traffic, 2) time and distance, and 3) personal comfort.

Often the straightest route was the most dangerous and least comfortable for the support team, but we needed to consider all of these factors, as the ride was as much a people event as it was a horse event. Some days we spent as much time scouting and talking to local residents as we did riding. Some scouting trips brought us in as late as midnight; then we needed to prepare for a 4:00 or 5:00 a.m. wake-up call.

It was raining every day now and Joyce wrote in her journal, "It is amazing how we go from L.A. to Texas without a drop of rain, and then we are hit daily."

Riding in the rain was miserable. The horses hated it, I hated it, and it was tough on morale. On September 11th, despite the rain, I covered 38.4 miles using both horses. We were going to try this extra distance every fourth day. Joyce wrote in her journal, "At this pace we will be in D.C. in no time flat." She mentioned the date of October 15th as our projected arrival date. On September 13, we crossed into Indiana. I was actually nodding off as we rode down a lonely rural road and missed a turn that I needed to take toward the Wabash River and the Indiana border. Brad had left us about an hour's ride from the bridge and was going to meet us there as we crossed into Indiana. When he arrived, we were nowhere to be found.

As Brad backtracked looking for us, he found where Highway 14 and Highway 1 met and then, several miles later, split off— Highway 1 went north on the Illinois side and Highway 14 headed east across the Wabash. Brad asked a man at the intersection if he'd seen a man riding a gray horse. The man pointed north up Highway 1 and there Brad found Ruler and me trotting along, going the wrong way. He drove up and said matter-of-factly with a straight face, "How's the ride going today?"

"Fine," I said, "Only thing is, I thought I should have crossed the Wabash by now. Maybe it's up around the next corner."

"Yes, maybe, if you were riding around the world, because that's the only way you could reach the Wabash by riding in this direction." Brad said.

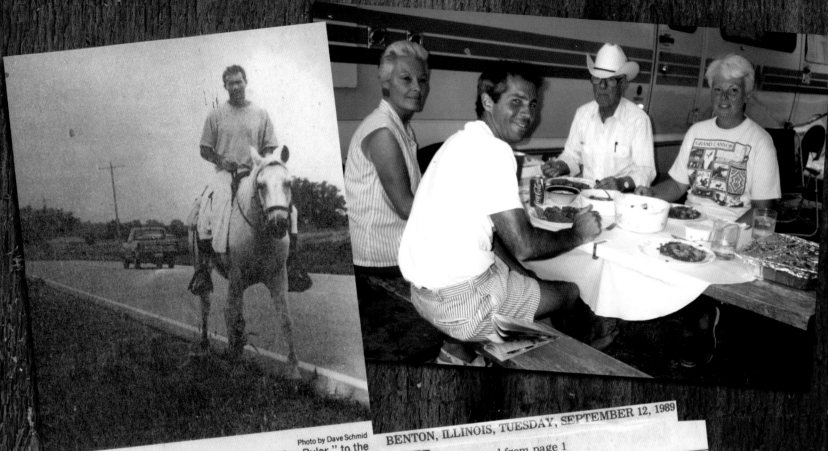

Photo by Dave Schmid

Lucian Spataro guides his Arabian gelding, "Sea Ruler," to the end of a day's ride east of Benton on Highway 14 Monday. He is riding across the nation to alert people about the harm being done to the earth's rain forests.

Rider travels nation to save rain forests

By Dave Schmid

In ancient times, Bedouin tribes of the Middle East trained these horses to endure the fierce desert sun.

This summer, a man is riding Arabian geldings across the country in an effort to save a very different part of the world from where these majestic horses were bred: the tropical rain forest.

The rider is Lucian Spataro, 32, a horse trainer from Tucson, Ariz. He passed through Benton Monday morning, going east on State Highway 14.

Spataro said he hopes

> 'It's a long, long way. Monotony kicks in.'
>
> Lucian Spataro, on 2,850-mile trip across United States

coast-to-coast journey will alert people to the dangers threatening the world's tropical regions, which comprise only 2 percent of the

See RIDER page 2

RIDER Continued from page 1

earth's surface, yet provide habitat for 40 to 50 percent of its plant and animal life.

Human beings are advancing rapidly on the world's rain forests, destroying an average of 50 million acres a year, according to the Rainforest Action Network, the California based non-profit coalition which is sponsoring Spataro's trip. At this rate of destruction, these dense and humid jungles will be erased from the map by the middle of next century, network members say.

Riding an average of 22 miles a day, Spataro has another goal. He wants to break the Guinness World Record for distance riding on horseback.

Since he left Los Angeles May 19, Spataro already has established a record for the longest distance and shortest time riding a single horse. He rode an Arabian horse a distance of 1,553 miles over the course of 63 days.

Since late July, Spataro has been alternately riding two Arabians, 6-year-old Sea Ruler and 12-year-old March Along.

He hopes to set another distance record when he reaches Washington, D.C. in mid-October, when he will have ridden 2,850 miles.

The long ride has taken its toll on horse and rider.

Spataro said his horses have been eating an average of 15 pounds of grain a day. Normally, they only eat three.

And Spataro admits that he sometimes has to fight off boredom. "It's a long, long way," Spataro said, "Monotony kicks in."

Donations can be made to the Rainforest Action Network, 301 Broadway 'A', San Francisco, Calif., 94133.

"Oh, no! Wrong way!" I replied with a grin. This was the first time in 2,000-plus miles I'd gone the wrong way. I turned around and rode all the way back, finally crossing into Indiana later than planned on September 13th. My little detour north up Highway 1 had cost us seven miles and about two hours riding time.

As I'd ride at night up to, through, and away from many large cities and small towns, I was always impressed by the glow I could see from miles away. I always wondered what caused that glow, and I was told that, as electricity feeds a community, it surges through the power lines, resulting in the twinkle you see from far away. It prompted me to think about the great amounts of energy we use in America. All that light is energy that comes from the earth as coal and is produced in coal-burning power plants.

In contrast to modern lights, while I was riding I could have been living in the nineteenth century, living a very low-energy existence of one horsepower per mile. The lonely ride caused me to reflect: "What if we really had to get from place to place by horse? Could society get along without petroleum, natural gas and coal? Could we replace them?"

Undoubtedly, yes, we will, with new technology. But when? When our present sources of energy become too expensive? This may not be in our lifetime or that of our children, but soon thereafter we will run out. As I look back now, I see very clearly that people tend to respond to a situation only when it hurts them financially.

Today, we have a double crisis on our hands of great significance.

First, we are still dependent on oil, gas, and fossil fuels in general, and the world's consumption is increasing, especially in developing countries whose growing economies are supported by the older carbon-based technologies. As we consume more, we jeopardize our future generations' access to these same resources.

Second, we are damaging the planet by consuming these products. We have the technology to produce fuel-efficient automobiles and homes, but we still don't have enough demand in developed and developing countries to drive down the cost so buyers can afford them.

When we as consumers demand certain products in the marketplace, the market will attempt to meet that demand. However, in most cases we are still demanding ecologically inappropriate products. Therefore, we consumers must focus on pushing alternative products that will improve our environment.

What people in this country want (and feel entitled to) is to have their cake and eat it, too. Until this changes, it will continue to be the basis of frustration among those in the ecology movement, which needs to be more closely linked to economic problems rather than to political ideology. We must bring the two closer together.

There's a new buzzword for the bundling of economic, social, environmental and cultural issues: "Sustainable Development." Seven years after my ride, I decided to accept the position of Professor of Sustainable Development at the University of Arizona to study these issues more closely, and to share what I have learned about them with the next generation of people who wish to support our environment.

ABOVE Chester, Illinois. Horses don't like crossing anything that is not solid. So now envision riding a horse over a very long, narrow, and slippery two lane steel bridge with a perforated surface that reveals the water rushing down below. You scout the bridge and cross in the early morning – with extreme caution.

OPPOSITE The magestic, timeless Wabash River flows along.

INDIANA, KENTUCKY AND OHIO

CHAPTER EIGHT:
THE ENVIRONMENTAL PARADIGM

ABOVE There is nothing better than riding into a brilliant, warm sunrise on a cold morning.

BELOW Lucian is trying to convince Brad that he knows where he is going as Brad, who is laughing about these directions, takes the picture.

OPPOSITE A tired and worn out team stop for a photo shoot in the cold damp drizzle of rain that is the Midwest in the early fall.

By September 14th, we were in Indiana. It was raining, and had been for about five days straight. I've included a picture one reporter took of Sea Ruler and myself that day. She had stopped to talk with us about the ride after she found us soaked to the bone, riding along a rural road in southern Indiana. It was raining so hard she would not get out of the car, but she did say she was excited to meet us and had driven 300 miles that day to find us. It was a miserable day for an interview, but the resulting article was very good.

Later that day, I sat in my trailer, feeling miserable. It was still raining and I had just completed the day's ride—23.7 miles. My trailer had been custom-built in the late '70s to transport and house both people and horses for a short period of time, at a horse show, for example. Before Al-Marah bought it specifically for this ride, it had been sitting idle in the back of a ranch in Arizona. To say the trailer needed some work was an understatement.

The Evansville Courier

Friday, September 15, 1989

15

TRI-STATE

He'll be back in the saddle for 900 miles

Rider makes horseback trip across America

By BETSY STANTON
Courier staff writer

SELVIN, Ind. — A man on horseback is no rare sight in rural Warrick County, unless you consider this trail ride has been 2,100 miles so far.

Lucian Spataro saddled up in Los Angeles on May 19 and wants to reach the East Coast by mid-October. His trek past the rivers and mountains of the United States is made in defense of another natural resource — rain forests. He's seeking support for the Rainforest Action Network based in San Francisco.

This week he carried his "Ride Across America" to Yellow Banks campground in Selvin, a resting place on the long ride he's taking coast to coast, said helper Brad Braden.

Spataro, 32, a blend of businessman, equestrian and environmentalist, planned this trip four years ago while diving in Mexico. After Spataro dove from a cliff, a friend asked him what his next feat would be. "I'm going to ride a horse across America," he said. Last year, he said he found the reason to do it.

RAN believes the destruction of tropical rain forests means the loss of up to 5 million species of plants, animals and insects and the chance to develop cancer antidotes from the forests' medicinal plants. It fears more than half the original forests have been destroyed.

Several corporate sponsors are funding Spataro's trip, including the Al-Marah Ranch of Tucson, Ariz., Spataro's hometown. The ranch provided Spataro's gentle Arabian mounts, Sea Ruler and March Along. With the aid of Braden

and Braden's wife, Joyce, who set up camp for Spataro along the way, he can change horses every day.

The Bradens go ahead of Spataro to set up camp, picking up horse and rider at the end of the day. The next morning, they return him to the place he stopped the night before.

At 20 to 30 miles a day, the trip is slow. "But how many people get to see America the way we're seeing it?" asked Braden, a semi-retired horseman.

Until he reached Oklahoma, Spataro rode mostly on interstate highways. More by choice, he's riding now on secondary roads, taking time to talk rain forests with the campers and passers-by who gravitate to the horses.

That's the plan, Braden chuckled. The animals are a good conversation piece. "Horses will draw people the same as they draw flies."

Larger cities are also hosting RAN fundraisers. At the end of the road, Spataro thinks his personal contacts will total 10,000 people.

The hardest part of the ride is mental, he admitted. After riding the first 1,000 miles on adrenaline, "it starts to kick in that there's still 2,000 to go," he said. "I try to stay alert, because the cars going by have a hypnotic effect on the horse and me."

Spataro has taken the road in breath-freezing cold, and desert heat that reached 117 degrees. He wore a yellow slicker Thursday to protect him from the misty rain. He's never had a serious illness or accident on the road, although both he and one of the horses tumbled down an embankment a few days ago.

Spataro hopes his ride also will earn him a place in the Guinness Book of World Records for time and distance. He's been in there already as part of a team of scuba divers who rode a tricycle 64 miles underwater in a pool.

Courier photo by BETSY STANTON
Lucian Spataro aboard Sea Ruler near Selvin, Ind.

INDIANAPOLIS

Ohio
River

MADISON

PRINCETON

NEW ALBANY

OPPOSITE Saddling up in the morning was a 15 minute ritual. Lucian would brush down the horse first thing each morning while Brad would religiously check the saddle and related tack to insure everything was in good shape for the day's 20-plus mile ride.

The living area was 10 feet by 20 feet and included a bathroom, kitchen, table and couch. The sleeping area was a shelf that jutted out of one side of the main cabin, with steps leading up to it. The major discomfort of the sleeping area was its size: although it was fifteen feet long it was only four feet wide. I was forced to crawl up into the sleeping cabin in the evening, and crawl out and dress down below in the morning. This had obviously been a real inconvenience when Sheryl and I had shared the trailer for the first 600 miles!

The trailer leaked, and the stove, heater and air conditioner did not work. We did not discover the air-conditioning malfunction until we were in Oklahoma, so it had been very hot in that trailer. The heater didn't work, either, so when it was cold, I'd had to heat the place each night by turning on all the gas burners for about 20 minutes.

However, since I didn't start doing this until we hit the East Coast, I only ran the risk of blowing up the whole trailer for about 20 days. A gas leak in the propane line could be why I slept so well at night those last 20 days—and why I was so groggy at wake-up time each morning at 4:00 a.m.

Now to the most difficult and disagreeable problem: the back of this trailer was a two-horse stall. I lived in the front, and the horses rode in the back. Although they slept outside in a pen, boy, was it smelly in the trailer! I was the only one on the team who could tolerate eating or just sitting in there because I had become accustomed to the smell. Most of the clothes I had on the ride still smell like horse manure!

It was really bad in the West and Midwest with the heat, and only got worse with the humidity and rain as we traveled east. The stench also attracted bugs into the trailer, and although it didn't bother me so much, we obviously couldn't do any interviews in my trailer.

This trailer, with all of its shortcomings, acted as our transport to and from our base camp and to our starting and stopping point each day. Thus, every morning I had to uproot and unhook my home, tie everything down, and load the horse or horses for that day's ride. Then we had to attach the trailer to the pick-up truck and head out to our stopping point from the previous day's ride to begin again that morning.

Eventually, we got this down to a science and could do all of it in less than 10 minutes.

Living conditions in Brad's and Joyce's trailer were considerably nicer. They had all of the conveniences of home, but in a much smaller version. While still a little cramped for a five-month trip, it wasn't all that bad.

Bob and Bea's digs, however, were a completely different story. They were traveling in high style, and their Winnebago was a home on wheels with a full living room, kitchen, dining and sleeping area. Bob had all kinds of video equipment, a veritable studio with a satellite dish on top and three television screens.

We certainly made an interesting caravan traveling down the highway or camping at a local campground!

Since I was up to my eyeballs in the everyday work of the ride, it did not dawn on me why morale was still so low. Bob and Bea had left the ride back in Missouri and would catch up with us again in West Virginia. Brad and I had aired our differences in Oklahoma and had come to some understanding; we were now voicing our opinions early on rather than letting our concerns build up. Yet, although this was working, it felt at times as though we were just going through the motions. I wasn't sure the team was going to hold together. We were all committed, but as time wore on, we were no longer enjoying the ride as we had in earlier days.

Of course, it was grueling—we had to endure early 4:00 a.m. mornings, bad weather and a demanding schedule of appearances and riding. It became apparent to me that if we were going to finish, we had to get back to having some fun, or at least acting as if we were.

In fact, that's the conclusion I came to while sitting in my trailer on September 14th. The rain was pouring down, my roof was leaking, and my back end was so sore I couldn't sit upright. I was not a happy camper. We'd been going about 25 miles per day, but we were losing ground and needed to ride more each day if we were to finish in October. Brad and I both knew this, but neither of us had suggested that we pick up the pace.

It was my problem. I was the person behind the ride and I was allowing us to coast. I may have been telling myself I was trying to pull together some energy for that last big push, but more likely my subconscious was saying: "Take it easy, relax." My body was really hurting and it was all I could do to get into the saddle each day. My enthusiasm was waning, and I was not pushing in the way I had been for the past 2,300 miles.

And unfortunately, my attitude was contagious. It was less apparent to everyone else that our low mileage was putting our mid-October finish in jeopardy, so I made a conscious decision to remedy the situation and work on improving morale. Any change had to start with me.

My renewed efforts to put things back on course worked, and gradually we all started pulling together again. We rode some 35- and 40-mile days back to back in the next fifteen days, and the back-to-back long-mileage days brought us back together and put us back on target for a mid-October finish. The day after I made the decision to try to boost morale, we decided to regroup to prepare for the next organizational and logistics nightmare. We had three more fund-raisers and media events to attend and we were about 200 miles, or a week and a half, behind schedule.

We were scheduled to be riding through Ohio and West Virginia in late September. With this in mind, Francesca had set up promotional events in Athens, Ohio, Harrisburg, Pennsylvania, and McLean, Virginia. If we had been on schedule, this would have put us in Athens in time for these events and then allowed us to trailer one horse up to Harrisburg for the fund-raiser from our route in West Virginia, as we had done in St. Louis.

But we weren't on schedule. We needed to attend the events without losing riding time, but we were still in Indiana. Taking the trailer back and forth each day to Athens and then Harrisburg would have added extra hours, tired the team and lost precious riding time. So we conferred with the Rainforest Action Network and decided to skip the Indiana section this time and do it later. Instead, we would trailer up to Athens and spend nine days there, using my father's home in Athens as a base camp.

Athens was right on our route. By following this plan, we could ride all of the Ohio route and a good portion of West Virginia. At the same time, we would attend the events in Athens and have a shorter trailer ride to the Harrisburg fund-raiser, as well. At the end of this nine-day stretch, we would then trailer back to Indiana to pick up the 220-mile stretch we had just skipped.

This new plan enabled us to ride the entire route without losing time and still attend the scheduled events. Operating out of our base camp in Athens, we would ride each morning and then trailer back to my father's place, from which we could attend various events. Each morning we would trailer out to our stopping point from the previous day and continue riding into West Virginia. This worked: during that stretch of September 15–24, we rode through all of the Ohio route and a big chunk of the West Virginia route and were still able to attend the fund-raiser in Harrisburg.

On the 24th we returned to our stopping point in Indiana and continued riding east. It took us eight days to ride the stretch from Huntingbird, Indiana, to just east of Cincinnati.

The coasting we did in Indiana just prior to this leapfrog was significant, as it allowed us to regroup and pull some energy together for what I would call "our last big hill"—the heavy schedule of riding and performing at fund-raisers before our final stretch to the finish. But it was great having a base camp for nine whole days!

Our ride into Ohio was an opportunity to put our issue in front of some people who I knew, from having grown up in this area, were on the leading edge of the environmental movement and would be very receptive to our message. Our media coverage in the college town of Athens, Ohio, was a bit more informed with Ohio University's student population who were already inclined toward environmental activism and more in-tune with where we stood on these issues from an academic standpoint.

The Athens NEWS, September 25, 1989 /5

OPINION

Now & Again

Rain forest rider opens some eyes

By Jeff Chappell
Athens NEWS Writer

I've often been criticized for being a cynical person. Friends, ex-girlfriends, parents, relatives, co-workers — I've heard it from every corner, and with just cause. They're right. From religion to relationships, my views are pretty grim compared to most.

But like most journalists I also have a streak of idealism — the world really sucks and I'm out to change it. Yet, in the daily grind of classes and holding down two jobs, sometimes I lose sight of it.

Occasionally, though, something happens to remind me why I got into journalism — why I hold two jobs on top of classes and worry about deadlines and gripe about sources and column inches. One of these somethings happened Sunday morning when I met Lucian Spataro.

As I stood on the berm of the Appalachian Highway on that cool, breezy morning and talked with this guy astride his white Arabian horse, I was taken by a sense of urgency in his voice as he spoke of the rain forests. My idealistic streak, which had lain dormant for a long time, came alive.

It came alive with good reason. This guy had taken a year — *a whole damned year!* — off from his life to ride across America to raise awareness of a problem that few people know much about but which most likely will determine the course of the world. Spataro's not making any money at it; he hasn't even raised nearly the amount of money he wants to donate to the Rainforest Action Network.

Granted it's something he has always wanted to do, but how many people would allow a year's interruption in their lives for a worthy cause and then not gain anything?

Furthermore, most people who hear about Lucian Spataro will probably forget about him and the plight of the rain forests by next month. (Here comes the cynicism!) They'll talk about it for a day or two at work or at dinner and then forget about it, as apathy takes over; it's just another problem the media blows out of proportion.

But perhaps a few people across the nation will have had their eyes opened. Perhaps even this column will incite someone to pay more attention to this issue and others.

Even if it's only one person, that would be worth it. It would make it worthwhile sacrificing a chance to party on Saturday night and awaking early Sunday — all to talk to Lucian Spataro on a cold, dreary morning. I can't speak for Lucian but I think he would agree that it was worthwhile.

You may not get a chance to read this, Lucian, and our paths probably won't cross again. If not, I'm glad I met you, and thanks for the kick in the idealism. Good luck with your part in changing the world. I'm glad I could help.

COVINGTON

Ohio
River

LOUISVILLE

LEXINGTON

OPPOSITE Our Letter From The Road, dated
September 21st. You can sense that we are firing on
all four cylinders now. The finish is clearly in sight, the
weather is crisp and clear, and we have been able to
hone our environmental message along the way with
positive results.

Alter we completed the route in Ohio and finished the fund-raising events in Athens and Harrisburg, we had a very depressing trailer ride back west to Indiana to pick up that 220-mile stretch we had jumped over. It was offset eight days later, though, by the exhilaration we all felt as we completed the stretch in Indiana and then drove all the way through Ohio and into West Virginia. Driving over the route we had just ridden two weeks before was great—it gave us a real sense of accomplishment. That was the first time in the ride that we had had a chance to retrace our steps after riding a major stretch.

The preceding article about us came out in the editorial section of an Ohio paper, and I believe it captured the essence of what we were trying to accomplish.

We also had some good news during this stretch. CNN had, in fact, picked up the ride and did two "Earth Matters" segments on our event. We also had some news that Willard Scott, the weather man on *Today,* was interested in our ride and might be able to meet us on the road to telecast a weather report. This would have been appropriate, as the end of this segment caught the last bit of Hurricane Hugo. Those two days were *not* fun riding!

How did we get Willard Scott's attention? Al-Marah had provided us with several thousand postcards of Sweet William and me to mail to people who might be interested. We had about 3,000 left, so in our monthly newsletter from the road we had enclosed a self-addressed card to Willard Scott.

Our letter from the road was going to about 2,200 people we had met along the way, plus many others. Upon receiving the card, these people were instructed to sign their names and write on the back where they were from, explaining that their friends were riding across the United States to raise money and to make the public aware of the rainforest issue. All of these cards were sent to Willard's office in New York.

However, Willard Scott also received a postcard at his home address in Virginia. As we were riding through Virginia, two supporters of our effort, Terry Dudis and Marie Ridder, had a fund-raiser for us. They invited Willard and his wife and sent him this invitation on one of the postcards. He probably thought: "Oh my God, now they've found my home address!"

Anyway, it did catch his eye, and he phoned that he could not make it, but that he was happy we were finishing. I was disappointed, but this was quickly offset by the CNN piece.

The fund-raisers in Athens were really impressive, with high attendance. The fact that the event was being held in my home town made things even more special. But most important, the people who attended were sincerely interested in the rainforest issue. The mayor of Athens, Sara Hendricker, proclaimed it "Rainforest Week" and presented the Ride Across America team with a city proclamation. We also had our first media event there at a place called the Dairy Barn, a restored dairy barn that had been a part of the State Hospital farm and now operated as a cultural arts center and meeting place in Athens.

That evening, the local ecology clubs put on a concert with local bands, and over 350 people attended. The feature act was by the band, "Barefeet," and my brother, John, was there

LETTER FROM THE ROAD #5   September 21, 1989

We are now in Ohio, with about 450 miles to saltwater. We plan to arrive about the 14th of October. It is a grueling part of the trek but we are all doing fine and are a bit pre-occupied with the finish.

We made a decision back in Oklahoma to run the event in two stages. Stage One would be a single rider and single horse going a distance of 1,450 miles in 69 days and an average of about 21 miles a day. At that point we would switch to Stage Two and finish the event with two horses. This would allow us to maintain our pace and fulfill our fundraising and speaking commitments on the rainforest issue. In looking back it was a very difficult decision to make but we feel it was the right one.

We are now riding Sea Ruler and March Along. Sweet William is back in Tucson getting a much deserved rest. Our riding schedule goes something like this: two days a week we go 40 miles, four days a week we go 29 miles and one day a week we go 16 miles. We are averaging about 210 miles every seven days. We average about 4 miles per hour. Not warp speed.

We had a good fundraiser in St. Louis thanks to Jim Volz's hard work. Thank you also to the Missouri Arabian Horse Asssociation and their generous contribution. The Ozarks were beautiful. We had a good fundraiser in Athens, Ohio with over 350 college students at a benefit concert with local bands. My father worked hard putting this event together. We then trailored up to a parade for the rainforest in Harrisburg, Pennsylvania and had over 100 people participate. The governor of Harrisburg proclaimed the week as rainforest week as did the mayor of Athens. Char Magaro was the driving force behind the Harrisburg event and I want to thank her for the effort and the party afterward. March Along sure did a number on Char's backyard.

We have had tremendous press coverage along the way with about five pieces on T.V. and fifteen news articles just since Oklahoma. CNN also picked up our event in Indiana and did a nationwide special on the rainforest and the Ride. They featured us with an ultralight pilot flying over Queensland to raise money for the rainforest cause.

It's great to be back in Southern Ohio. It is now fall and the trees are beginning to change color. We began in spring and have gone through summer and are now into fall. We just hit Hurricane Hugo and will be riding through torrential rain for the next few days.

It amazes me that we are close to the finish. It has been a very long, difficult but deeply rewarding five months. This will be the last letter you receive from the road. However, you will hear from us at the end of the event. We are assembling a booklet of our press coverage along the route with a map and pictures of the start and finish and various areas in between. We will finish the Ride in Virginia or Maryland just south or east of Washington, D.C. We all say hi.

Lucian signing for Sea Ruler, March Along, Brad, Joyce, Bea, Bob and Francesca

(415)
398
4404

301
BROADWAY

SUITE
A

SAN FRANCISCO
CA 94133

Lane Larson gets in a little reading on the train (with Scott Davis sleeping) while riding to our drop off point near Mexico City.

ABOVE Lucian at 14,500 feet (or thereabouts) on the north face as the storm blows in.

OPPOSITE Lucian at 11,000 feet on the three day 25-mile trek to base camp and (inset), Lane Larson and Lucian at the HASE expedition base camp, 12,700 feet on the north face of Mt. Orizaba.

playing guitar. The band was actually very good, and it was the first time I had been able to watch my brother in action. I was impressed. It gave me a different perspective on John, since he and I are very different. He's 12 years younger than I am, and I think I'd still pictured him as the little brother I used to pick on at home. He'd grown quite a bit and was taller and bigger now, so picking on him then was out of the question.

John really didn't think much of my endeavor to ride a horse this far, but he did show an interest in the horses and always stood outside the house petting or just watching them. By now many things I do that are a bit unusual don't faze John much. I think he and other members of my family have come to accept that I periodically go off and do something crazy.

I remember my first mountain climb for a Guinness Record scuba attempt at high altitudes, which really put my mother and father into shock. However, over the years they got used to activities like these. My father worked hard for us, setting up different fund-raisers and speaking engagements in Athens. He was very supportive and didn't question my motives or my decision to attempt the ride. I had spoken to him during the planning stages and we discussed the trade-offs of undertaking an event like this.

I remember speaking to him about the personal and economic sacrifices necessary, and his comment was: "If you are going to do it, finish the job." He even promised to buy me dinner at Tucson's most exclusive restaurant, The Tack Room, when I finished the ride. Come to think of it, he still owes me that dinner; unfortunately, 20 years later, the Tack Room is no longer in business.

I had been back in Athens for a day here and there in the past twelve years, but only to drop in and say "hi." I never had much time to spend there, however, and would quickly leave and head back to Tucson or California. The response from the Athens community in general was great. Even some of my old high school friends who were in town showed up at the fund-raisers. It was nice to see them again and they were very supportive. Looking back on my Athens years now brought a flood of memories as both a young boy and then a young man—a lot of nice memories.

Athens was a town with a character all its own. I remember coming back there in the early '80s and finding a phone booth where you could still make a ten-cent phone call. The city had many brick streets, and the main street of the town was about 400 yards long.

The town is perched up on top of a series of small hills and surrounded by the Hocking River, making it much higher than the surrounding area. When I was a child, the Hocking River would often flood, and the town would be surrounded by a moat. Since that time, the town built a by-pass that brought most of the traffic around the city and the U.S. Army Corp of Engineers rerouted the Hocking River so it didn't flood the town anymore.

The campus of Ohio University dominates the downtown area and is still the lifeblood of the community. Today, Ohio University has about 18,000 students and the town doubles in population when school is in session. With all the college activities, Athens has enough to do

Handwritten annotation: MT. ORIZABA HASE Expedition 4/87 Mexico

Tucson Citizen

Monday, January 12, 1981

Local men plan volcanic lake dive

By JAMES R. WYCKOFF
Citizen Staff Writer

A Tucson team of adventurers plans to leave soon for Mexico and hopes to scale a snow-capped, 18,700-foot volcanic mountain and send a couple of its members on a record plunge into a lake.

The group of local divers and climbers said it has chosen Orizaba, the third-highest peak in North America, as its target and plans on launching its expedition by Sunday or next Monday.

Climbing the mountain will be no easy task. But simply reaching its top, officially 18,701 feet above sea level, is just a secondary goal.

Known in Aztec times by the name of Cit-laltepetl, the mountain was first scaled in 1848. It last erupted in 1687.

What the young Tucsonians, all in their 20s, are really shooting for is the high altitude dive, which they believe would set a world record.

"Not even the Navy has ever dived that high up," said expedition business manager Lucian Spataro, 23.

Tucsonian Lane Larson, 26, who has been experimenting with high altitude diving, as has Spataro, will lead the effort. He will be joined by other Tucsonians, Scott Davis, 22, Doug Powell, 20, and parttime local resident and freelance writer Mike Stoklos, 29. Another Tucsonian may also join the climb, members said.

Besides the normal camping and climbing gear, the group will have to lug a variety of diving equipment and special respirators up the mountain. Members have trained for months by running with full packs on in the Santa Catalina Mountains, they said.

A base camp will have to be set up at about 13,000 feet, and at 14,000 feet and up, team members anticipate needing oxygen masks and sulphur-protective respirators.

Orizaba, Southeast of Mexico City and west of Veracruz, is one of a string of volcanic peaks along the Plateau of Mexico. Spataro said it is "semi-active and belching sulphur," thus the need for special respirators.

Group members are willing to endure that problem because it is a side effect to the volcanic heat that keeps the lake from freezing over despite its altitude. Most lakes so high above sea level probably never will be explored by divers because they are frozen year-round, team members pointed out.

Only three people are expected to make the dive and they will spend no more than four or five hours at the crest because of breathing problems. Members don't know what they will find at the lake — it could be five feet deep or hundreds of feet deep, they said. They will need a variety of diving gear because they will need to improvise at the scene.

Members said they hope to find out about the effects on divers of entering water at such an altitude. Diving is tricky at high altitude because the effects of nitrogen on divers' bodies at various high points is not what it is at sea level, Spataro said. The Navy's diving tables to help divers avoid the bends are based on dives at sea level, and the team hopes to "adjust" those tables for high altitude.

to keep a youngster occupied and in just enough trouble to keep life interesting—especially for parents.

The day after the reception at the Dairy Barn, my father set up several speaking engagements at local schools where the horses and the team members and I loved to go. Children are so sincere and so interesting to speak with, and so much more mature nowadays than I was at their age. I think their exposure at a young age to technology and the media have allowed them to mature faster than my generation did. These kids are working on technology at the age when I was barely able to swing a bat and add and subtract.

The presentations went over very well and I think the horses enjoyed the attention from the children as much as we did. It was as if they knew they were the honored guests, and the kids enjoyed the chance to pet each one.

It was late in the day on September 17th, and Brad and I decided to go out for a last-minute ride, covering about 13 miles. Every mile counted. The total that day was 39.5 miles. We had done 27 in the morning and then 12.5 that night. We were keeping up the pace and covering the distance, despite the events we were scheduled to attend each day. These were very long days for us all, and we would ride, trailer to an event that afternoon, trailer back to our route and ride some more, then back to our base camp and sleep. It was very demanding, but enthusiasm was high and we were really chalking up the miles!

Along the miles of road I had ridden, I had seen many hundreds of billboards. These, like television ads, newspaper ads, and radio jingles, bombarded the public to buy, buy, buy, consume, consume, consume. It seemed to me as I looked at all those ads, that economic progress had brought on a frenzy of consumption. And it's become easier to buy a new product when an old one breaks down—and cheaper, as well, given soaring repair costs and lower retail prices.

Today we bear the consequences of a "throw-away society," along with the accumulation of huge, unnecessary amounts of solid waste. We are literally burying ourselves in our own waste. There are not enough landfills to hold the staggering amounts produced every day.

As I rode through my home town of Athens, Ohio, local environmentalists and concerned citizens were trying to block the dumping of garbage from New York in Athens County. There were numerous articles and extensive media coverage about this issue, but a United States Supreme Court ruling states that garbage is a commodity, and states cannot refuse to take out-of-state waste. Therefore, the landfill operator could legally accept waste from New York as long as the out-of-state trucks continued to pay the nominal dumping charges.

On the other hand, I was happy to see the progress Athens had made regarding the collection of recycled material. As we were using my father's home as a base camp, I could see the response on recycling day. Almost every driveway on Strathmore Boulevard was piled high with bundles of newspapers, sacks of aluminum cans, cardboard and glass.

The recycling program in Athens not only cut down on the amount of solid waste but it also provided employment and income after the recycled materials were sold. I spoke to Tom

OPPOSITE If you are an environmentalist, Athens, Ohio was and still is Nirvana; the community has been on the forefront of environmental activism for decades. I can remember as a youngster growing up in Athens – the environmental protests that were held on the college green back in the '70s and late '60s, and then later the community participation in the clean-up that was done in the region to reclaim strip mine projects and stone quarries.

COLUMBUS

Ohio
River

MARIETTA

CINCINNATI

JACKSON

OPPOSITE With traffic that you can reach out and touch, Sea Ruler is now immune to the sights and sounds of the road and has matured into a steady partner who Lucian can trust on these very narrow two lanes roads that were our primary route now, as we cross this part of the country.

O'Grady, the brainchild behind the Athens Recycling program, and found that the program was growing quickly. In 1989, Athens' recycling program processed 1.5 million pounds of material. In the first 6 months of 1990, the center did over 1.3 million pounds. In the year 2010, the Athens recycling program had grown dramatically and is more than just a recycling program. Today, it is both a recycling and conservation program and the focus on both has significantly reduced the per capita waste generated by the community.

In Athens, some strong local leadership and several small grants were needed to get them started, but when I rode through it was nice to see neighbors outdoing neighbors as they placed their recyclables on the curb every other week.

Back in 1989, many cities that I traveled through showed little evidence of attempts to recycle. Apart from the issue of waste, litter was still a problem in the United States. In 1989, as I rode along highways and rural roads, I was often knee-deep in trash. We always had to be very careful of glass fragments along the sides of roads, and especially in California, this was a major concern. I couldn't help wishing we were back in the days of refundable bottles. If people could get money back on their glass bottles, perhaps they would be less inclined to throw them away.

On September 19th—still on the Ohio leg—I rode 27 miles in the rain and crossed the Ohio River at Parkersburg, West Virginia. I rode another 20 miles into West Virginia. We were now on U.S. Route 50, which I planned to ride all the way to the coast. Brad picked us up and we drove back to Athens to shower and change. Then we drove the 380 miles to Harrisburg, Pennsylvania, for a scheduled fund-raiser.

Brad and I got there very late, about 10:00 p.m., and met Char Magarro, RAN's East Coast coordinator, who was hosting the event. After we set up the pen for March Along in Char's backyard, we proceeded to hit the sack—we were truly exhausted.

The next day we got up early and drove down into Harrisburg to meet 50 other riders. March Along and I, and Brad—on a borrowed horse named Hi Windsong—led a parade of about 150 people and horses through downtown Harrisburg and into the state capitol of Pennsylvania. We met representatives from the governor's office and had a rally on the steps of the capitol as various speakers talked about Pennsylvania's environmental commitment.

Randy Hayes, the director of the Rainforest Action Network, flew in to speak as well. He was just in from New York and had been at a meeting with United Nations Secretary General Xavier Perez de Cuellar. At that meeting, he had presented a worldwide petition with 3.5 million signatures, wheeled into the UN in 100 grocery carts. The petitions included 600 thumbprints from natives living in the Penan Rainforest of the southeast Asian nation of Borneo—then under attack from Japanese and United States logging interests.

The petition called for a United Nations special session on the rainforest issue. Randy was pleased with the results and spoke to the crowd about the importance of grassroots groups like the Rainforest Action Committee of Harrisburg.

Brad and Lucian riding Ruler and March in the back of the Save The Rainforest parade.

OPPOSITE Governor Casey rolled out the red carpet for the Ride Across America team. His proclamation and the related ride through downtown garnered quite a lot of television and newspaper coverage.

These groups, Randy said, were needed to mobilize the public worldwide and put pressure on politicians and corporations. A letter-writing campaign to Burger King resulted in a cancellation of more than 35 million dollars' worth of orders for Brazilian beef, he said.

After speaking, I was presented with a letter from the governor of Pennsylvania, Robert P. Casey that endorsed and supported our efforts. Despite the long drive to Harrisburg and the pressure it had put on our schedule, we were pleased with the results. We had received significant television and newspaper coverage for our cause.

I also saw my family. My uncle, Carl Spataro, who lived in Harrisburg, took a day off from work to walk in the parade, to my delight, and later that evening and the next day I visited with my aunt and uncle, whom I hadn't seen in more than 20 years.

The most enjoyable activity, however, was the party that Char had at her place that evening for all the participants in the parade. Brad got a chance to play some basketball with Ona, Char's daughter, who was quite an athlete. (He lost.)

We woke up early the next day, the 21st of September, to drive down into Gettysburg for another round of fund-raisers. We thanked Char and Ona for their help in organizing the parade and we took off with the understanding that they would meet up with us again at the finish. We got to Gettysburg only to find that our fund-raisers had been cancelled as a result of bad weather related to Hurricane Hugo. Brad and I spent the night in Gettysburg and then drove back to Athens the next day. The three-day break from riding was great and we got back to Athens fairly fresh and ready to hit the road again.

On September 23rd, we rode 25 miles farther into West Virginia and then drove back to Athens. That evening we had a farrier come out to look at both horses, reset their shoes and replace their Easyboots. That evening, we broke camp at my father's place and prepared for our trip back to Indiana to pick up the 220-mile stretch we had jumped over.

We got into Indiana at about 4:00 p.m. on the 24th, set up camp and went to bed. I slept straight through till 6:00 a.m. the next day. For the first time, we had overslept on the ride! This showed us how tired we all were from the last nine days of riding and fund-raising.

COMMONWEALTH OF PENNSYLVANIA
OFFICE OF THE GOVERNOR
HARRISBURG

GREETINGS:

As Governor, I welcome you to our Commonwealth and extend congratulations on your efforts to increase America's environmental awareness through Ride Across America.

In Pennsylvania, we are striving to save our environment through investing in clean water, recycling and toxic waste cleanup.

Our legacy as a state and as a people rests on our ability to clean up the environment. Our quality of life depends on the standards we set for ourselves and future generations. Just as we share great expectations for our children, so do we share the responsibility of giving them a better world.

Three of the major concerns we face as a world are massive deforestation, ozone depletion and global warming.

Our rainforests provide us with 25 percent of all medicines in United States pharmacies; they are also the single largest source of oxygen. But at the rate they are currently being destroyed, tropical rainforests will be gone by the year 2050.

We have a long way to go in our fight to repair the damage done to our resources, but through education and awareness, especially of our young people, we can rebuild the environment.

I support your efforts to raise environmental awareness.

Best wishes.

Robert P. Casey
Governor

During the next stretch, I rode 29.2 miles on the 25th; 41.3 on the 26th with both horses; 36 miles on both horses on the 27th; 18.5 on the 28th; 31.3 miles on Sea Ruler on the 29th; 25.2 miles on two horses on the 30th; 22.5 on the 1st of October; and 23 miles on the 2nd of October.

We were now east of Cincinnati. Our route crossed the Ohio River at Madison, Indiana. I then rode into northern Kentucky staying south of Cincinnati, crossed the Ohio River again, and then rode up east of Cincinnati to Route 32. We now had joined the previously completed Ohio stretch. Over that last stretch in Indiana, we averaged 28.4 miles per day, our best stretch yet, so Indiana hadn't turned out to be the tough state we'd anticipated.

On October 2, we broke camp and drove across Ohio and into West Virginia, driving across the route we had just ridden. We were now at a base camp in Grafton, West Virginia. We would ride the stretch east and west of Grafton and then on to Virginia.

A day later, the leaves were just beginning to change color. It was cool at night and the rain had finally stopped. Athens had been a turning point. We'd had some fun, but we'd achieved a lot, too. I had been able to go home for a little while and spend some time with my family, and the town brought back some good memories.

But there was one incident in Athens that was not so positive.

We were east of Athens on Highway 33 as I rounded a bend in the road and found myself face-to-face with a four-car collision that must have happened only seconds before. One man was trying to both direct traffic and pull people from the cars. Two cars were overturned and one was on its side. This was not a pretty sight, as there were probably ten people in the four cars.

I quickly dismounted, tied Ruler up, and began directing traffic to allow the other man to pull people out of the cars. He was clearly overwhelmed, and soon we both were. I felt we should leave several of the victims in their cars until more qualified help could arrive. I certainly didn't want to move anyone without the proper equipment, so I convinced my fellow rescue worker to concentrate on which victims could move without injuring themselves further. Just as we began to assist them, several ambulances pulled up, so I went back to directing traffic.

I was soon relieved of my traffic directing duty by a police officer, who asked me some questions. As I hadn't seen the accident, I couldn't answer them, and with nothing else to do, Ruler and I rode on.

About twenty minutes later, a police officer drove by and thanked me for the help. He told me ten people had been involved, including my rescue buddy. In fact, he may have been the cause of the pile-up! Three people were okay and six were hospitalized, while two were seriously injured.

About five minutes afterward, my father pulled up, clearly shaken. He'd feared that I had been in the accident, so he'd driven out to check. He was relieved to find out that we were okay and still riding toward West Virginia. He took some pictures and went back to Athens, reassured that his son was still alive. He'd also driven out to bring me some inserts for my running shoes, and I was deeply touched: he'd made an 80-mile round-trip drive for a $1.00 pair of inserts. I hope I am as committed to and supportive of my children as my parents have been to me.

OPPOSITE Heading east into early morning fog, on Route 32. Also known as the James A. Rhodes Appalachian Highway, it is a major east/west route from Cincinnati, and we picked up this road to Parkersburg, crossing the Ohio River into West Virginia.

WEST VIRGINIA, VIRGINIA, WASHINGTON, D.C. AND MARYLAND

CHAPTER NINE:
THE FINAL STRETCH, THE APPLE CART AND THE FINISH LINE

ABOVE and BELOW Lucian and Sea Ruler "on their game" riding toward Grafton and some hot apple pie at the 4 Corners.

OPPOSITE To Brad's dismay, Lucian and March Along have found a short cut.

Being in Grafton, West Virginia is a heck of a lot easier than getting there. This is one difficult town to find and maneuver around. Grafton is situated at an elevation of about 1,200 feet among very craggy mountains. I don't know how else to describe the terrain except to say, "it's rough." It reminds me a lot of the mountains coming out of Albuquerque—very sharp and deep, with plenty of tree-lined valleys, steep hills and clear, cold streams. The horses and I drank out of the smaller streams along the road.

I had heard that there were many caves in the area, and it wasn't surprising, given all the high plateaus and ridges that appeared to slope in all directions at once. Some were gradual, but many were steep and even precipitous. There were also many rock formations and frequent vertical and overhanging cliffs. As we rode through this area, we found ourselves going up and down these ridges—very seldom were we on level terrain.

Ohio
River

GRAFTON

PARKERSBURG

OPPOSITE Grafton in the '30s and '40s was a town built into a mountain; in 1989, those small narrow roads were still challenging for a guy riding into town on a horse.

Fall had descended upon the Appalachian Mountains and the leaves were beginning to change color. Previous logging and farming had contributed to a great diversity of the vegetation in this area. I saw primarily white oak, both red and sugar maple, shag bark hickory, black oak, beech, and walnut. Most of these trees were located along the ridges and slopes, and changed colors throughout the fall. The image of these ridges was often like a rainbow and, as we rode through the area, the rainbow changed as the terrain and the vegetation changed.

There were also many deciduous shrubs and smaller understory trees interspersed throughout—redbud, sassafras, flowering dogwood, apple, and maple. I saw a lot of paw-paw, an edible fruit, and huckleberry and spice bushes.

The fragrances in the fall were overwhelming. The trees and the cool, clear air and cool, clean water dazzled my senses—touch, smell, taste, sight, and hearing. Everything I viewed was in razor-sharp focus. The deeper I breathed in, the clearer those images became.

The weather was just getting nippy, and when we were riding into Grafton, we ran into a dense fog bank and got separated from the vehicles. We had agreed to meet in the 4 Corners Cafe if we got lost, but riding through a fog bank at night in a small unfamiliar town with narrow, one-way, very slippery streets made me more anxious to find the cafe.

When I got there, I discovered that it was closed for the night, but because it was right in the center of town, none of us had any problem finding it. Brad and Joyce came in about one hour behind me and did the same—they found 4 Corners closed and then proceeded to the same gas station I had for directions to the Grafton city park, our next base camp.

We stayed at the park, just east and south of the town under the Tygart Lake Dam. This was actually the largest cement dam east of the Mississippi, with a solid cement base 200 feet wide. The park sprawled along the river, which seemed to originate below the dam. Getting to the park by horse on the small one-way streets and narrow two-lane roads was challenging. Brad agreed, calling it "a very slow and humbling experience."

Before 1960, Grafton had been a glass-producing town, with the Hazel Latis Glass Company as a major business entity. In the '30s, '40s and '50s, it was also a railroad switching and repair center for the B&O Railroad, and later, for the CSX railroad companies. The rail and glass industries were the principal employers those days in the valley.

All of the homes and some of the businesses were propped up on the hillsides or set down in the valley bottom. Many narrow one and two-way streets meandered around the residential areas and then into the main part of town, connecting the outlying areas with the downtown area. For someone unfamiliar with the city and the one-way streets that seemed to go on forever, this could be a dizzying experience.

Residents claimed that Grafton was the final resting place for the first Yankee buried in the Civil War—T. Bailey Brown. Grafton is also the location of the first organized observance of Mother's Day, which took place in the Andrews Methodist/Episcopal Church. There, on May 10, 1908, Anna Jarvis led the first Mother's Day service ever held. They no

Carr China Co.

MANUFACTURERS OF

VITRIFIED CHINA

HOTEL. ROLLED EDGE. SPECIAL DESIGNS
CRESTS & MONOGRAMS

Grafton, W. Va.

longer hold regular services each Sunday in the church, but they do have a Mother's Day service each year.

Bob and Bea rejoined the team for the final stretch on October 3rd and we all went out to celebrate with dinner at the 4 Corners Cafe, appropriately named as it sat at the juncture of Route 50 and 119, forming four corners. There, I ate the best food east of the Mississippi and the best hot apple pie and homemade ice cream in my life, with the exception of my mother's apple pie, of course.

On October 5th, as I was riding into the outskirts of town, Brad pulled up next to me and told me to stop. I did, and found out that just around the bend, in front of a small cemetery and war memorial, was the site of an unforgettable accident. Two months before, a young lady named Claudia Von Ostwalden and her horse, Max, had been traveling west along this same stretch. They were struck by a truck driven by the manager of a dealership in Grafton. Claudia was uninjured, but the horse could not go on. This horse and rider team had been attempting to set a record by crossing the United States on horseback.

I found out later that the young lady was, in fact, trying to race us across the United States! From what I understood, she had seen an article in a magazine about our ride and had left the East Coast soon after we'd left the west coast. I estimated by her pace that she had ridden 350 miles during the same time period we'd covered 1,100 miles. I also found out later that she rode through Athens, Ohio on her second horse, Sport, while the first horse was still in Grafton recovering from the accident.

Apparently, Claudia had stopped somewhere just shy of the Texas border. Her timing was off; she had wanted to reach Oregon in September and was still in Ohio in late July.

While doing my research for our ride, I had learned that our chances for success would be much better if we rode west to east, primarily for two reasons. First, I knew the ride would be toughest, physically and psychologically, out west with very few people and long distances between the various communities. I also knew that adrenaline and energy early in the event would carry us over these physical and psychological hurdles.

The last thing I wanted to see, with ebbing energy and unfocused eyes, was thousands of cold and windy miles and countless horizons still to go. So going east to west was out. I knew we would need, toward the end of our journey, the moral support and the additional stimulation of the more populated eastern cities and towns.

The second reason was that it would be much easier to endure heat than cold. So by riding east from California, we could pick up the very early warm spring days in California and Arizona, and this would give us basically five to six months of good riding. Going east to west, we would not have had that same luxury. It was still very cold in the east in May, but even more important, riding east to west at our estimated pace would have put us in the west during October and November. Riding through those windswept stretches in New Mexico, Arizona, and California in the fall and early winter would not have been fun.

OPPOSITE Grafton is your classic small American town, warm and friendly. A scene from "Back in the day," a Sunday at the 4 Corners in Grafton.

I had come to the conclusion that the only way to do the ride and catch the best of all three seasons was to begin in May in California, and then ride as fast as possible, hoping to reach the East Coast in late September or early October.

This young lady had done just the reverse and was riding much too slowly. At her pace, she had probably caught the first blast of fall weather somewhere just shy of Texas and decided to call it a day. She still had the windiest and coldest stretches left to go. I wouldn't have wanted to be riding through that area during the winter, or even in the fall.

Brad told me he had found out all about Claudia's accident when he was parked in front of a Ford dealership looking for some water for the horses and some touch-up paint for the truck. He had walked into the dealership with his boots and cowboy hat and, as was often the case, he was hit with some questions about Arizona because of our license plate. He then started telling everyone within earshot about the ride and the rainforest issue (Brad was really getting the lingo down now on the rainforests).

Before he could go any further, he heard one guy say, "Well, that means we'll have to keep ol' Tom here off the roads until you and your rider get through town." It seemed that Brad was talking with the manager of the Ford dealership, who had actually driven the truck that struck Claudia and her horse. So he had gotten the real scoop "from the horse's mouth," as they say. The horse that got hit, by the way, was still in Grafton and was doing fine.

Traveling down Route 50 in the fall from Clarksburg to Virginia and on into Washington, D.C., is a trip I will never forget. It was spectacular in the fall with the leaves changing, and as we drove at the break of day, we could see mist rising up from the many rivers and streams that paralleled and crossed the route. I loved seeing the wildlife at every turn.

Growing up in Ohio, I'd always told travelers that West Virginia was, and I believe still is, the most beautiful state east of the Mississippi. It is within a stone's throw of many major metropolitan areas all along the East Coast, yet remains somehow primitive, isolated and unaffected. It is a place from a different time and reminds me a lot of the Ozarks.

Small towns, with little more than a hardware store, cafe, and gas station, dot the route, each significant for a different reason. The route as we rode into Virginia brought up visions of the Civil War, Lincoln, and the fight against slavery and oppression. There were landmarks everywhere identifying various battlegrounds and homes of gone, but not forgotten, heroes and citizens. The people in these small communities clung to the history of the area and spoke of the various happenings as though they had only occurred yesterday.

For me, it was a step back in time. Each town—Gormania, Redhouse, Mt. Storm, and Junction—had been named for very practical reasons. "Junction," for instance was a real junction, a trailhead of sorts from years ago. "Redhouse" boasted a prominent red house near the center of town. Often the prominent family in the region got to name the town, sometimes for a family member, usually the father of the first clan to settle in the area. These were very practical reasons by very practical people.

OPPOSITE A valley overlook in West Virginia is also a look back in time and relatively unchanged in 100 years.

October 6th was a nasty day for riding. It was cold, with sheets of rain and wind blowing in every 15 minutes. Even March Along, who was usually able to adapt to bad weather, had his tail between his legs and his back to the wind. Luckily, we were riding with the wind and it was going to be a short day, only about 22 miles. This was all very steep terrain, high mountains and deep valleys, straight up and straight down. The road was very slippery. March Along had Easyboots over his steel shoes on his front feet only, which helped as we were riding down the mountains, but didn't give us much traction going up.

This particular stretch was even more treacherous because one very large mountain began deep in the valley, rose for four miles and then descended for six miles. The Cheat Mountain had 52 very narrow switchbacks on the way up, making it a very, very dangerous road for a horse and rider.

A "switchback," for those unfamiliar with the term, is a trail's abrupt, often very tight shift in direction. The idea behind a switchback is to make a climb easier. Rather than going straight up the mountain, the trail meanders back and forth, switching direction and climbing very slowly. As a result, it took us more than two hours to make the climb. The problem was compounded by the fact that Route 50 continued to be a major truck route into the East Coast.

On this particular day, as we rode over this very narrow two-lane road in blinding rain, I counted 103 trucks in the ten-mile stretch up the mountain and down the other side! There aren't many places on such a narrow road for a horse and rider to move away from traffic. When a truck would pass another on a switchback, I could actually touch one because they were going very slowly. I wanted to keep my hand on the trucks and on the horse in case I needed to push off to gain some more distance. Over the guard rail to our left or right was often a sheer drop-off, and the other side of the road offered nothing better, typically a sheer stone cliff rising up from the road.

There was literally no place to go. Luckily, the trucks were going so slowly up the mountain that they often saw us and made a real effort to avoid coming too close. In such weather conditions, however, the drivers sometimes couldn't even see us, and we had several very scary encounters on this ten-mile stretch.

On the morning of October 7th, Bob and Bea caught up with Sea Ruler and me in Gormania. I needed to make a phone call to a Detroit radio station and took the opportunity to get some hot coffee and some fresh apple pie at the Country Cupboard Cafe. It was about 65 degrees outside and would eventually reach about 75 that day—a perfect day for riding. I made my phone call to Detroit and also made a phone call to Al-Marah in Tucson. With the time difference, it was about 8:00 a.m. in Tucson. I had already been up for seven hours.

The coffee wired me—in fact, as Bob said later, it was as "black as the bottom of the pot," but it tasted good and warmed me up inside real quick. In fact, I was on the phone with the radio station when it hit. That caffeine had me talking so fast, I was literally shaking and actually had to stop the interview.

OPPOSITE The "game plan" for the climb up the Cheat was don't look down, back, or up. Just keep moving forward and up, one step at a time.

Later, I spoke to a doctor about this. He said that the caffeine (which I was not used to) combined with the small amount of food I had eaten and my body weight of only 143 pounds had generated a response similar to an allergic reaction.

(Now, when I drink coffee, I drink it diluted half with water, and usually iced.)

That day, I rode 29 miles, mostly out of the saddle as a result of the caffeine. After riding through a small corner of Maryland and then back into West Virginia, I wrote in my journal: "We are very close now, and it's as if someone were dangling the carrot and just gave me the first nibble (Maryland)."

I told the rest of the crew how I felt when I got back to camp. They all seemed excited, too, as if we could smell the finish line up ahead.

On October 8th, Sea Ruler and I climbed out of a four-mile-long valley and up onto a ridge about 1,900 feet high. Somewhere on the top of this ridge between Junction and Romney was a lookout that pointed south. There was a sign for "the Nancy Hanks Memorial," the mother of President Abraham Lincoln, who had been born nearby. From this high vantage point, I could see nothing but a tree-lined valley off into the horizon. It's rare to find such a panoramic view in the east. While out west, one gets used to seeing the sun set or rise on a beautiful horizon. After a while, you might even begin taking the scene for granted. But here in the east, after riding for months without a view like this, Ruler and I stopped and just stood there quietly for 20 minutes, looking over the magnificent landscape, before we rode on.

For most of the ride that day, I was preoccupied with plans for our ride through Washington, D.C., and the final route to our finish. I had made several phone calls that day in the small towns I rode through, trying to reach Charles Applebee of the Maryland Department of Transportation. I would reach the receptionist and Applebee would be out. The secretary's first response: "Would you like to leave a message and a number where he can reach you?"

My response: "Tell him I'm the guy riding the horse across the United States and I'm 120 miles from Maryland and riding his way. I need him to clear a route for me to the beach."

"You must be kidding," she replied.

"No, I'm not. I'm dead serious. He'll remember me. I spoke with him six months ago. Please tell Mr. Applebee to stay in his office tomorrow until 9:00 a.m. I will call him then from my horse."

She must have thought I was crazy.

For some reason, I had delayed defining and clearing the final route to the beach on the East Coast until the last two weeks of the ride. I had spoken with both the D.C. and Maryland people a month before the ride began, but we could not put together a final route over the last 75 miles.

While still in Tucson, I hadn't known how we were going to ride through D.C. and on to the beach. On the west coast in L.A., I'd had a chance to peruse the route, but on the East Coast, 3,000 miles away, I told myself (knowing better), "We'll just play the last 125 miles by ear to add a little excitement." I didn't know until about four days before the finish the exact route I

OPPOSITE Sitting on the top of the ridge in quiet wild solitude is important, for no other reason than to inform our understanding of our connection to these wild places that once fed us and shaped who we are today. The view from the Nancy Hanks memorial.

would take to the beach. Because of the maze of small streets and roads and small towns in this area, I had thought we might just sneak on through—which is actually what we did!

It worked fine until we got pretty close to D.C. This was horse country anyway, and we were on Route 50, which doesn't require permits. In the rural areas between towns we didn't stand out much, but we still had to contend with all the small towns and municipalities. I had timed it so I could ride through them all in the early morning or sometimes after dark.

However, at this point, I just didn't have the energy, the time, or the patience to deal with bureaucracy for the set of permits on the last 125-mile stretch. I remember saying to myself in Tucson, "I'll deal with this last stretch when we hit Virginia, and when we make it that far, nothing will keep us from riding into the coast. We'll Rambo our way in!"

It turned out that this last stretch did involve a little "Rambo-ing" and a little bit of bluffing, too. I rode every bit of the way, but I did get stopped several times. In downtown Fredericksburg, I had to fib and bluff a bit. I told a police officer that I had a permit, but that if he stopped me to look for it, our ride would be delayed, jeopardizing a major media event. I then told him the whole story about the ride and gave him and his buddies a brochure.

In all cases, the police let us ride on through—in this case, with a police escort, no less. It made me wonder about all the time and energy I had put into getting the other 60-plus permits for the first 2,800 miles. Had it even been necessary? Could I have just bluffed my way across the United States? Or were the officers so taken by our determination and confidence at this point that they assumed without question that we had permits, or we could not have gotten this far? I was betting on that.

Now, Washington, D.C., was a different story. Route 50 went right into D.C., and rather than take the road right to the Lincoln Memorial, I rode through residential areas and even through Arlington Cemetery—with a police escort!

Bob Shepard had begun working with the D.C. police about five days before we were to ride through. We actually had only one permit for D.C., which we took with us. Because of all the earlier encounters we'd had with police precincts on our way to D.C., we suggested that they call each other and help us coordinate our ride through the area. This boosted our credibility and implied that we had a permit for each precinct through D.C. to the Maryland border.

When we used this strategy, the question of permits never came up. As the precincts coordinated with one another, each assumed that we must, in fact, have legitimate permits, so they simply passed us from precinct to precinct.

We found out, as we were riding through Washington, that we actually needed a total of seven permits for the D.C. area, including one for the White House lawn. But we just kept on riding. We had some media coverage, which helped to legitimize us and gave us additional credibility. I've included a map of our detailed route through Washington and then around the Capitol and the White House and on down Pennsylvania Avenue.

Going The Distance For The Environment

Arizona activist starts cross-country ride for the sake of tropical forests.

By Jennifer Johnson

Concerned environmentalist Lucian Spataro and the Arabian gelding AM March Along will spend the summer crossing the United States in order to increase public awareness of the plight of the world's rain forests. Spataro's goal is to raise more than $1 million to aid preservation efforts. Corporate sponsors are providing the tack and gear, while Bazy Tankersley, of Arizona's famed Al-Marah Ranch, offered the sturdy gelding in support of the cause.

Seeing this country by horseback as our forefathers did a century ago is a dream of many equestrians. For Lucian Spataro, a 31-year-old business consultant from Arizona, it will begin to become reality early this May when he and a 12-year-old Arabian gelding start their approximately 3,000-mile trek from Los Angeles to New York. Spataro is hoping to set a world record for the longest ride made by one man and one horse, but there are also serious purposes to his pursuit. Along the way, he and his four-legged companion will be raising money for the preservation of the world's tropical rain forests and providing scientific data on the effects of long-distance riding.

Three years ago Spataro began toying with the idea of making a transcontinental ride. As a teenager, he participated in local ride-and-tie and endurance races. He also took pack trips with his horse, often spending several days at a time out on the trail. Riding across the United States seemed to be the natural next step in his equestrian challenges, and his increasing concern for environmental issues prompted Spataro to join the cause with the adventure. "I decided that if I was going to spend 800 hours in the saddle, I should do it to benefit the rain forests or some equally deserving cause," he explains.

Spataro set the wheels in motion by contacting two environmental organizations—the Rainforest Action Network (RAN) in San Francisco and the Environmental Policy Institute (EPI) in Washington, DC —to gauge their interest in his idea. Both organizations were receptive since they rely on contributions to support their efforts to save the fragile forests from the ravages of industrialization and the pressures of growing populations in the third world. "There is a tremendous amount of potential here," says Randy Hayes, a representative from RAN. "This could raise quite a lot of money for the rain-forest projects."

Finding sponsors for the ride and a loaner horse capable of going the distance proved to be less difficult than Spataro had expected. Corporate sponsors have provided the tack and gear necessary for the ride, and Arabian

The map shows Potomac River, Winchester, Arlington, James River, and Richmond.

OPPOSITE Lucian and Sea Ruler, doing 27 miles, closing in on Washington D.C.

Our bluff didn't work with Mr. Applebee of The Maryland Department of Transportation. He knew I had no permit for Maryland, but he also knew that I knew I was not required to have one if I rode on any Maryland thoroughfare that wasn't listed as an interstate.

By this time I had become very familiar with most of the state laws on this subject, and Mr. Applebee agreed to outline a route using rural roads and state four-lane highways on into Chesapeake Bay. He got the route approved in no time flat, and we were now all set, from Pennsylvania Avenue east of the capital to Chesapeake Beach, Maryland.

On October 8th, we continued our ride down Route 50; we were then camped at the Cherry Hill campground in Winchester, Virginia. I had come down off the ridge where Nancy Hanks had been born and had ridden into a long valley. At the bottom, I found a small hotel and made a phone call to Leslie Barclay to get directions to a small dinner she was having in our honor the next evening at Val Cook's in Washington, D.C. I got the directions to the hostess' home and told Leslie I would see her the next evening. That day I rode 28.3 miles on Sea Ruler.

October 9th was clear and cold. I scraped ice off the truck window that morning, and we had no cloud cover behind us. I'd learned that a clear night, when you can see the stars, is going to be a cold night no matter what the location or season. Cloud cover seems to lessen the cold and humidity makes the air seem warmer. I had used the gas burners the previous night to heat the trailer and finally, I slept well.

Then, I had ridden 29 miles, showered and changed clothes for the dinner. When I put my clothes on, I really looked skinny—not thin, but skinny. Nothing fit and I felt like the "bag monster."

I had dropped off my jacket, pants, and shirt at the dry cleaners in Winchester so I wouldn't smell as though I had just ridden in wearing them to the dinner. How many people go off to a party in Washington having just ridden in on a horse? I laughed as I realized that this could make for very interesting conversation at the party. I walked out of the trailer and flash bulbs began going off. Bea and Joyce were having a heyday with me. Neither had ever seen me dressed in anything other than running tights, boots, or jeans, with the exception of when we were in St. Louis, when I wore jeans and a jacket. Now, clad in a blue blazer, khaki pants, white shirt, red tie, set off by a nice tan I had earned on the road, I left for the party.

After parking our pick-up truck between a Mercedes and a Jaguar, I noticed I still had some hay and horse manure in the back of the truck. I hoped no one would notice, and proceeded to have a great time at the party, where I talked to lots of people about the ride and the rainforests. I met Val Cook's daughter, Diana, an avid rider, and some other very interesting people, and finally got back to my trailer park about 2:00 a.m.

I wrote in my journal that morning: "The next day is not going to be fun." I was right—it wasn't.

I always like to do my longest rides in a daze, when everything seems to fade by. On this day, October 10th, I had a 38 to 40 mile ride planned using two horses. I started out on

Sea Ruler and rode 20 miles, and then Brad brought up March Along, so I put in another 20. I was fading fast on two-and-a-half hours' sleep, and then, unbelievably, it started to rain! I still had ten miles to go at 4:00 p.m., so I cantered March Along for three of the ten and then began walking one mile and cantering a half mile, walk one, canter a half. I couldn't have felt more miserable, and to top it off, I didn't have my rain gear with me, so I was soaked to the bone.

The excerpt from Bob and Bea's journal that day reads:

"Tuesday, October 10, 1989, Bob and I took off after Bob made some phone calls for Lucian. Things are winding down now. We met up with Lucian about 20 miles out, he was beat, poor puppy! He was riding two horses today to cover 40 miles. We pulled into a driveway where Brad was waiting. Somehow we missed seeing that huge trailer on our way out. When Lucian rode up, Brad, Bob and Lucian looked at maps, planned timing and checked the route. March Along, who had been waiting in the trailer and was now saddled for the last 20-mile stretch that day, began nudging Lucian as if to say, 'Let's get going, it's going to be dark soon.' Lucian asked Bob to make a few more phone calls for him. If Lucian could have his laptop computer on the horse, he would work on that, too…"

I wrote in my journal that day: "This was the toughest day since Texas." I also wrote: "And this is the last tough day. I took a big chunk out of the carrot today. We are really going to make it."

Just before going to bed, I did an interview with Dr. Bob Hieronimus of the *Dr. Bob Show* on the American Radio Network. The talk show lasted 50 minutes, and I did it from a cold pay phone in the Candy Hill Campground. We had seven call-ins on the rainforest topic. I was one of three on a panel answering questions about the ride and the rainforest.

At the end of the show, Dr. Bob asked the radio audience a question about the ride. If someone knew the answer they could call in and win a t-shirt and video. He asked what kind of horse I was riding across the U.S. One man called from Ohio and said it was a white horse. Wrong—no prize. And then a lady called from Florida and said they were Arabians, and she won. We finished the show and I hung up and went to bed. Another long, long day was over.

On October 11, 1989, 1 saddled up at Rectors Crossroads, where Mosby's Rangers fought. John Mosby was known as "The Grey Ghost" in the Civil War. This stretch of Route 50 was known as the John Mosby Highway, in memory of the Rangers. Route 50 was also an important commuter route to D.C. By chance, I always seemed to catch some part of rush hour. This highway was like a large, long, four-lane parking lot in some places, so instead of riding the edge I would ride right down the road between traffic lanes.

I caught quite a bit of attention as I did this, and that gave me the opportunity to pass out brochures right off the horse as people rolled down their windows to ask me what the hell I was doing out there. What a great way to break the ice!

Earlier that day, while riding through Upperville, I passed an apple cart at a vegetable stand on the side of the road. The man was selling three different types of apples. I stopped and asked him if I could have an apple for my horse. I only had fifty cents on me to make

We rode this route like "The Grey Ghost," moving in and out of the early morning fog. Drivers had to blink twice as we rode on by, like the Rangers did one hundred years ago.

phone calls if necessary and I didn't want to spend it, so 1 told him I didn't have any money on me. He gave me two bruised apples from the back of the cart. I ate one of them.

What will bring a smile to your face is sitting on the side of the road after a long ride and sharing a big red apple with your horse and just contemplating it all.

The 9:30 a.m. traffic was slow, so there wasn't much action at the apple cart. We sat there for a few minutes watching the traffic go by. It was a really nice fall day, about 70 degrees with sunshine and bright fall colors everywhere—a great change from the previous day. I was sitting there thinking how close we were to the finish, how happy I was to complete the ride and how much fun it had been. I was thinking about all of the funny things that had happened along the road, kind of laughing to myself, a little bit dazed, just staring off after the cars, when the owner of the apple cart made a comment about my riding attire and saddle.

"You don't look like any rider from around here," he said,

"Now why is that?" I asked curiously.

"All these riders from around here ride in English saddles on big brown and black horses and look like they just came out of a magazine for some clothing and saddle company.

It's disgusting. Now you look like you've put some miles on that saddle, and the way you're dressed it looks like you're prepared to go a few miles more."

I took a real hard look at myself. I had on Nike 990 running shoes with tattered shoe laces, and small burrs in the laces, probably from as far back as Texas. I had two pairs of running tights on, white over black. I had holes in the white ones so you could see the black tights coming through behind the knees and in the crotch. I had on white ankle socks and a purple bandanna around my wrist and another around my neck. I was wearing a shirt and had a sweatshirt tied to the saddle.

The shirt was a "Save the Rainforest" t-shirt, primarily white with a color illustration of the rainforest on the front and back. The shirt had recently been washed, but had grass stains and grease marks on it that even Tide could not get out. My sweatshirt was black and tied with a piece of leather to the saddle. The sweatshirt hung down the side of the saddle dragging one arm against Sea Ruler's front right leg.

Yes, altogether, I must have made quite a fashion statement!

I took a look at Sea Ruler, sweat stains coming down all four legs to his ankles. He was a little dirtier than usual, because he must have rolled last night. We only brushed him up in the morning under the belly and on his back, where we put the saddle. That kept those areas clean and free of abrasions, but the rest of the horse looked pretty grimy, especially when the sweat mixed with the dirt from the roll the night before. It was hard to get all the spots off each morning in the dark, and we hadn't found out how dirty he was until the next day after I'd already put in five to seven miles in the dark.

This morning, I had been riding in some tall weeds and had obviously picked up some big burrs that had tangled in his mane and tail. We were a bedraggled pair and, as the man said, looked as though we had put on the miles.

I had just finished my bruised apple and Ruler was nudging me for another, so I gave him the core, which I usually eat, seeds and all—good roughage. I was still hungry and the man said, "You want a really good apple?"

I said. "Sure, but so does my horse. Can you afford it?"

He went rummaging around in the back and brought out two of the largest apples I'd ever seen. They were as big as my hand and I had to cut them in half for Ruler to be able to bite into his half. We sat there talking for a while longer and I knew the inevitable question was going to come up. Finally he asked me, "You aren't from around here, are you?"

"No, we're not. We're from Arizona."

He laughed and said sarcastically, "Looks like you rode from there, too."

I turned to him slowly and in a very serious and deliberate manner, said, "We did. We rode the whole way from Arizona and we just got here today."

He stopped laughing to see what else I was going to say. I waited about five seconds—seemed like an eternity—and then laughed and said "No, I'm just kidding. You'd have to be crazy to ride a horse that far."

He laughed with me in agreement and said. "You're right, darn straight, you'd have to be plumb loco to ride a horse that far. I thought you were serious."

I said, "No, I'm not that crazy," and turned to tighten up the cinch on the saddle.

"You want another apple?" he asked.

"No, I've got to get going."

"Stop in any time for an apple."

"I'll do that. See ya later," I said and rode on.

Ten days later, I drove by that same apple cart on my way back west in a Hertz rental car. I stopped to get an apple. As I got out of the car and walked up to the apple cart, the same guy walked up from the side of the stand. I looked into his eyes to see some glint of recognition.

There was none. He didn't recognize me at all.

"What kind of apples are you looking for?" he asked.

"I'm looking for an apple for my horse."

It took him about five seconds and then a big old smile lit up his face from ear to ear. He said, "I didn't recognize you dressed in a nice jacket and not on a horse."

I said, "Yes, but I still want an apple, and I have money to pay for it now."

"It's on the house," he said and went in the back and brought out the big apples again.

"How do you ever make any money at this if you give all these apples away to people who ride by on horses?" I asked him.

"I don't see that many people ride by that I would give an apple to, and besides, I don't need the money. I just do this for fun. Where's your horse?"

I told him he was resting at a farm in Poolesvllle, Maryland.

"You rode him all the way to Poolesville?"

"No," I responded. "We trailered him up there and I'm heading back to Arizona."

"I thought so," he said. "Poolesville's a long ride; must be 75 miles from here. I thought you might be riding that horse back to Arizona."

I laughed and said to him, "No, you'd have to be pretty crazy to ride that far."

He laughed and said. "You're right, darned straight, you'd have to be crazy," and quietly added, "It'd sure be fun though. Have a good trip."

October 12, 1989, and disaster struck when our truck went out for the full count. We were just preparing to ride the stretch to the Potomac River and across the Memorial Bridge into D.C. that day. But the truck's catalytic converter died, and to ride my horse 2,900 miles, we had put 9,000 miles on that truck, trailering back and forth. We still had to go 2,500 miles back to Tucson.

I spent the whole day in the Ford truck shop waiting for the truck to be repaired. They completed the work at 5:00 p.m. under warranty, thanks to the Jim Click dealership in Tucson, who'd donated the vehicle. Then, we were on our way.

I drove back out to pick up Brad and Joyce and found Bob and Bea there with the media. Bill Pollard, owner of the house we broke down in front of was, interestingly enough, a previous owner of Al-Marah horses, and he knew of Bazy and the ranch. He gave Joyce and Brad some lunch and called the media people, who arrived there about the same time I did. We did a few interviews and hooked back up and drove on to our last base camp in Maryland. We would return the following day to complete our ride into the Potomac. Our finish on the 14th would have to be postponed for one day.

At the time it was very frustrating, but looking back, things really worked out well. This allowed us to ride through D.C. on a Saturday, rather than on a busy Friday with traffic, and the new time worked better with our last fund-raiser.

On October 13, 1989, I rode the 31-mile stretch just west of the Potomac, rode across the Potomac and into what I considered D. C. to the Lincoln Memorial. We hit major traffic from 6:00 a.m. to 9:00 a.m. Two newspapers caught up with us along the route, the *Faquier Democrat* in Warrenton, Virginia, and the *Loudon Times-Mirror* in Leesburg, Virginia.

Riding through bumper-to-bumper traffic, passing out brochures like a modern-day Johnny Appleseed, does attract attention. I was actually making better time than the cars I was riding past.

This was Friday, and we finished the first part of our ride at the Lincoln Memorial. Brad had March Along with him, so we unsaddled Sea Ruler and loaded him up. Then we drove through D.C., past the White House and on up Pennsylvania Avenue to a point just east of the D.C. city limits. We unloaded March Along and saddled up, and I continued riding another ten miles toward Chesapeake Beach.

We had six miles to ride in the D.C. area, from the Lincoln Memorial to the White House and then past the Capitol and east out Pennsylvania Avenue. We had left the last four miles to the beach, giving us a total of ten miles to go. We had arranged it this way so we could ride the D.C. piece early Saturday morning and be available to attend a fund-raiser in the evening. We would catch the last four miles late Sunday morning, ride into Chesapeake Beach, and finish at about 1:00 p.m.

On Saturday, October 14 at about 7:00 a.m., we were all set to ride into D.C. We were scheduled to meet some press people in front of the White House at 10:00 a.m., so we had some time to do a dry run. We drove the route with Brad so he'd know where to meet us at each press stop along the way. We wanted the trailer and the banner in as many pictures as possible.

There were tourists, joggers, and demonstrators everywhere. We had several photographers and a TV station catch up with us at the White House, around which I rode, and then on up to the Capitol where we stopped for some photographs.

We soon found out that we were not allowed on the lawn, and since we did not have a permit for that specific jurisdiction in D.C., the authorities threatened to confiscate March Along and arrest us. The encounter went something like this:

ABOVE and OPPOSITE Brad, March Along, and Lucian in D.C. The problem with solving the environmental crisis is that the issue does not grab and hold our interest on a global basis, and for this reason we aren't able to recognize collectively the danger that is imminent. As is so often the case, the environmental issues share center stage with a host of other concerns and in D.C. we found that to be especially true, where on our day media time was shared with numerous other groups competing for coverage.

Arundel Newspapers Photo/Victoria Bellarose

Lucian Spataro and horse travel on U.S. 50 at Upperville.

Ride across U.S. comes to Catlett

By MARK SCOLFORO
Democrat Staff Writer

CATLETT — Lucian Spataro celebrated the end of his record-setting horse ride across the United States at a fundraiser in Catlett Saturday, but still termed the trek a qualified success.

Spataro rode 2,780 miles in 116 days to bring attention to the problem of rain forest destruction in Central and South America, a subject about which he said the public is too ignorant.

He estimated that he talked to about 75 people each day of the ride, and many of them knew little about the problem.

"On a scale of one-to-10, I'd call this a 7.7," said Spataro Saturday, at a fundraiser organized by his childhood friend, Terry Dudias, at Cedar Lee Farm. "I wanted to set the record and draw attention to the issue, and we did both of those."

On the fundraising front, however, Spataro said the $100,000 he raised for the Rainforest Action Network was "a little shy."

He hopes that the judges at Guiness World Records will accept the first part of his ride as the record for the longest trek by one rider and one horse. After that horse was unable to contine, Spataro finished the second half of the ride with two others. All three horses are Arabians.

He began in Huntington Beach, Calif., during rush hour, and ended in Chesapeake City, Md., on Oct. 15. The ride, said Spataro, was one-fourth boredom, one-fourth panic, one-fourth strange and one-fourth interesting.

At the fundraiser in Catlett, Char Magaro of the Pennsylvania branch of the Rainforest Action Network gave a brief talk to the 30-40 people assembled there.

"The whole purpose of the Ride Across America was to elevate awareness among Americans why we need the rain forest for a healthy planet," said Ms. Magaro.

"One-half of our original tropical rain forests have been destroyed. The rain forests keep an ecological balance on our planet," she said.

Rain forests are being destroyed at a rate of 50 million acres a year, an area the size of England, Scotland and Wales.

Destruction of the rain forests may influence climate, the ozone, and availability of certain rare pharmaceuticals.

Spataro said he wanted "people to realize that there is a group of people putting a lot of energy into something," so he devised the Ride Across America as a publicity stunt.

The money he raised during the ride, which itself cost about $60,000, will go toward Rainforest Action Network projects in Central and South America.

The last leg of the ride was along U.S. 50 from Ohio through West Virginia and into Fauquier County at Paris. He finished up by crossing Memorial Bridge after stopping in Arlington National Cemetary.

"A lot of things can happen up here as a result of deforestation," said Spataro. "We really don't know their impact — we're involved in a type of experiment."

Ms. Dudias got involved after she read an article about Spataro in Equus magazine, and remembered him as her brother's best friend during their childhod in Ohio.

She contacted him through the Rainforest Action Network, and asked her to produce a fundraiser for him while the team passed through the area.

"I hadn't been very aware of that a serious protem the rain forest issue is," said Ms. Dudias, "but the more I learn the more I think it's an important issue."

(Editor's note: For more information about the rain forests, write The Rainforest Action Network, 301 Broadway, Suite A, San Francisco, Calif. 94133.)

A big security officer and a little security officer walked up to us as I was trying to position March Along for the *Equus* photographer. You know, on those TV shows like "Candid Camera" the photographer keeps telling the subject to back up a little more and then a little more, until finally the subject backs right off a cliff or falls over a chair or some other obstacle. Well, our obstacle was that duo of security officers. The photographer had his face in the camera and kept asking me to back this way and that way.

Little did I know that two officers had come down from the White House to see what we were doing, riding around the White House lawn. They positioned themselves right behind March and didn't say anything to me or the photographer for a minute or two. I didn't even know they were standing behind me, so I kept backing and backing until I heard a very loud, "Ahem, excuse me."

I wheeled March Along around to find ourselves face-to-face with the two officers. I noticed in the grass below that March Along's last step backward was just inches from them. March Along was now nuzzling the little officer, who was doing everything he could to defend himself and remain professional. I could tell he wanted to let his guard down, but he couldn't

OPPOSITE March Along and Lucian in D.C. In the past, the U.S. has demonstrated that we have the wisdom and strength to identify and rise to the important challenges, and we have made the sacrifices to make the world a safer place. In this environmental crisis, that burden once again, rests with us, those whose footprints step hardest on this planet.

BELOW The route through D.C. and on to the beach was a mix of state routes, side streets, and Pennsylvania Avenue.

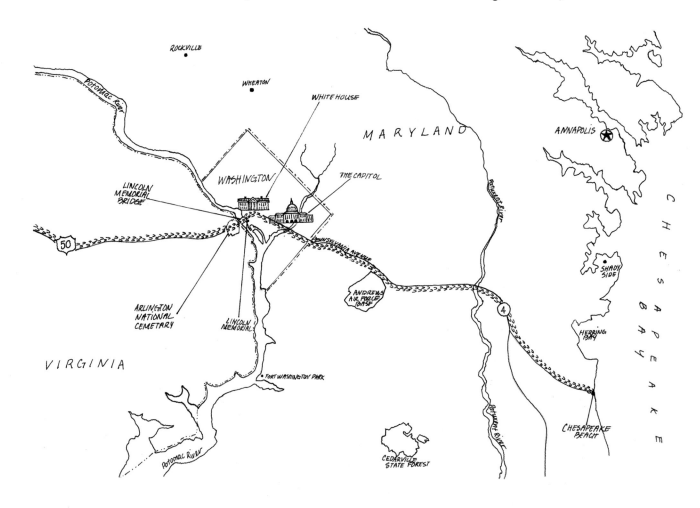

BALTIMORE

WASHINGTON DC

CHESAPEAKE
BEACH

Chesapeake
Bay

OPPOSITE Lucian on Sea Ruler and Brad on March Along, 2,963 miles later, sharing a well deserved celebratory ride on the beach in Maryland.

because the other officer was still drilling me with questions. March Along, however, was persistent and continued in his search for a carrot or some other handout.

Both officers finally gave in to his persistent head-butts and began petting him. I pleaded innocence, that we hadn't been informed by the police earlier. They finally relented, and other than this glitch, no one really paid us much attention. That was understandable, since that same day on the lawn in front of the Capitol there were four different demonstrations going on. In a sense, we were number five, and each of the demonstrators considered their presence a very big deal. But media-wise, we got only token coverage.

Still, we were very happy with the results. That evening, we had a fund-raiser in Catlett, Virginia with Terry Dudis, a high school friend of mine from Athens, Ohio. Terry had read about the ride in *Equus* magazine and became an enlistee in our effort. She and Marie Ridder, a member of our board of directors, offered to have a get-together and celebration at the finish. This event was to occur on the last day of the ride, but because of the truck failure and our one-day delay, the celebration turned out to be one day early. I wasn't complaining—we'd had a good turnout and good media coverage. It was a fitting public finale.

We gave some awards out to the team members, Brad and Joyce and Bob and Bea, had some cold drinks and had a very relaxed time. Terry had a one-acre grass paddock where the horses had a chance to stretch their legs. This was the first time in five months that they were free, not confined, and they spent at least a half-hour running, kicking and cavorting in the pen while all the people at that party stood and watched in awe. It was a real show. They were running so fast that Sea Ruler actually threw off his Easyboots! I had planned to ride him the last four miles into the beach the next morning, so we put them back on.

I was glad the finish was the next day because it gave me a chance to complete the ride in a more private way with the people who really helped make it happen.

On Sunday, October 15, we awakened at about 8:00 a.m. We only had to trailer about ten miles and ride four; no big deal—a piece of cake. Everyone was pretty calm and quiet: it seemed like a pretty normal day on the ride. We got the horses loaded and drove to the drop-off point. Brad and I rode in the truck with the horses, and everyone else went on to the beach. If I trotted most of the way, it would only be a one-hour ride.

As Brad and I drove down the road, not saying a word, it felt strange. It would be the last time that we would drive together like this—and neither of us could say a word. I wanted to say so many things, like, "Thanks for sticking it out; you made it happen; I learned a lot from you," and on and on. But nothing came out.

We had done this same drive many times over these last five months, and while we were so different in personality, we were very similar. I broke the ice by saying—what else— "Well, this is it."

Brad replied. "Sure is. It's been a long road."

I agreed, "Yeah, that's for sure," and we both laughed.

OPPOSITE When thinking about this problem it is inconvenient and often uncomfortable to ask the question that you must ask, which is, where do I stop and nature begins? The conclusion you will eventually come to is that there is no distinction and when you come to this realization, it is at this point you will begin to understand who you really are and how your perception of this world and your role impacts our behavior toward these natural systems.

But then I said, "It's been fun," and Brad said, "Same for me." That was it. That pretty much summed it up.

Back in camp, we had agreed to take a shortcut to the drop-off point. It wasn't well marked, and, believe it or not, we got lost. On the last day, four miles from the beach, we could not find the drop-off point I had marked the day before.

We backtracked and came down the road on a more familiar route and quickly found it. Despite the 30-minute delay; we were still a little ahead of schedule, and Bob was waiting for us at the drop-off point. When we finally pulled up, he found Brad and me arguing over whose fault it was that we'd gotten lost. I was arguing and laughing at the same time and I think Brad was as well. Even so, he was putting up a good fight. I remember saying. "I can't believe it. After all this time, we get lost on the last day."

I'm going to win this last argument, though, because I have the last word, and the only way Brad can get in the last word is to write his own book. Here it is— the last word: Brad missed the second turn coming out of camp.

There, I did it. Although maybe— and that's a big maybe—I didn't see the turn.

Now we were at the finish. We had been riding for 150 days. We'd gone 2,963 miles. What could I say? It was an intense challenge that required every bit of mental and physical energy I could muster every minute of every day. I had wanted it that way. I had wanted to feel the sun and the wind and the heat and the cold. I had wanted to be on an emotional and physical edge. I had asked for that challenge.

I kept the tension level up, and by offering an example, I had asked the other team members to maintain a high level of concentration for the duration of the event. We had accomplished that ride under very difficult physical conditions over a very long period, and we stretched every aspect of the ride to the limit. We'd stretched ourselves both physically and mentally. We also stretched our horses, our equipment, the media, those who helped; we pushed very hard, and now, on the verge of finishing, I was filled with relief. We'd made it, we'd beaten the odds and had persevered and we'd gained the cooperation of so many others.

I had written in my journal in Missouri: "I feel a growing burden to finish, and it emanates from those who've helped. We are now riding for these people. They are the real reason I keep riding."

The rainforest is a very important issue: it has long-range global implications and is, I firmly believe, one of the top three most pressing environmental problems facing us today. But what is most important is how people relate to this crisis and how effective we are at convincing people of its importance.

I continue to believe, as I did when I began that ride, that the best way to convince someone you are sincere and that you care is through your example. We cared enough about this issue to take on this challenge, and ultimately, to finish. That to me is the example I want to leave with you.

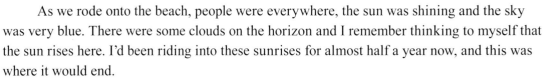

OPPOSITE *(from left to right)* The TEAM,
Joyce Braden, March Along, Brad Braden, Bea
Shepard, Sea Ruler, Lucian, Bob Shepard. At
the finish on the beach in Maryland, October 15,
1989. 2963 Miles in 150 days.

BELOW Lucian and Sea Ruler whooping it up
a bit at the finish.

As we rode onto the beach, people were everywhere, the sun was shining and the sky was very blue. There were some clouds on the horizon and I remember thinking to myself that the sun rises here. I'd been riding into these sunrises for almost half a year now, and this was where it would end.

Brad was holding March Along, and Sea Ruler must have known something was up—people were hollering and yelling congratulations—because he had his tail up, which he'd never done before, and his ears were bent forward. He saw that big old body of water and must have thought, "No way am I going in there."

I thought of Sweet William's first step into the ocean on the West Coast 150 days earlier. It seemed like so very long ago. At this point in the bay, there were no real open areas—it was all private property, built up with condos and residential housing. To get to the beach we had to get the permission of a condo owner to ride on through the property and over a small rock retaining wall; then we were in the water.

All of the condo people were there to wave us on through. I smiled as we passed them on our way in. Then, someone poured champagne on me and Sea Ruler, and Bea gave me a big kiss. We all got together and made some videos and did some final interviews. I took some pictures with my Aunt Katie and Uncle John, and Uncle Chuck and Cousin Lenny, who had come in from Alexandria to see the finish. My father had driven in from Ohio, and it was great to have all of them there. Everyone was in very good spirits.

Brad and I rode both horses into the water and up and down the beach for quite a while; we gave Char and Ona, who'd arrived from Harrisburg, a ride. Then Brad and I shook hands, and that to me was significant. Brad had been a key element in the ride and had contributed to our success. He'd managed those horses as no man I knew could have done, constantly playing the odds, the trade-offs between injury, distance and fatigue. Like a conductor of an orchestra who knows just when to use the right instrument, he played those horses like a master.

Bob and Bea, Joyce and Brad, and the horses and I, got a chance to thank each other on video. Bob and I talked for an emotional minute and then drank some more champagne. I took off the cowboy boots I'd worn when I rode into the water, and I've never worn them since.

At the finish I felt as if a big burden had been lifted from my shoulders—and was then replaced with an even heavier burden. As I was riding the last mile to the beach, I said to myself, "I can't let this end here. I need to build on this and the discovery I made back in Texas, that you truly never really fulfill your commitment to making this world a better place in which to live."

This commitment became my new burden. I remember actually thinking about that as we were riding into the water. Perhaps an excerpt from a letter I wrote to one of our board members captures the essence of my feelings during the last moment of the ride: I feel it sums up my thoughts right after the event far better than I can now.

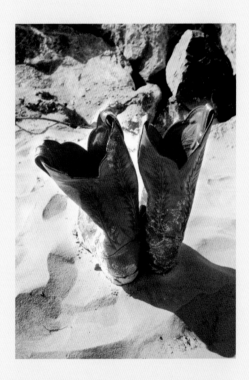

We are officially "boots off, feet up" celebrating on the beach in Maryland. Bazy once said, when referring to this ride, "In this race to finish is to win." As I look back now these words ring true for the environmental movement as well. We are on this planet for the "Long Ride" and with this in mind, we aren't yet at the finish.

(An excerpt from a letter, November 8, 1989)

To A Board Member:

"Well, we made it. One year to the month after first talking to you. 150 days on the road and 2,963 miles. It has just now begun to set in. In looking back, I am really happy to have had the opportunity to do the ride. It was not always apparent to me during the event that we were really accomplishing something of great significance.

The ride did not turn out to be the event that would shake the world and awaken the world to the cause. In almost a desperate way, I wanted it to be that event and I tried very hard to meet all of the expectations and objectives early on. By the time we hit Texas, it was apparent to me that it was not going to be the event that I wanted it to be and that if we were going to finish I would have to concentrate and focus all of our energy on the most important aspects.

At that point, the evolution of this event took its most significant turn. I began to focus on the people we met along the way and in a sincere way tried to convince them that the cause was important. I put a lot of energy into getting accurate press coverage on the issue.

I also discovered that the desperation I felt came from my own feeling that this would be my last hurrah, and that after completing this event I would have fulfilled my commitment to making this place a better world. When I discovered that this was not to be the case and that you really never fulfill that commitment, I began to enjoy the event a lot more and was less desperate.

That discovery did not come a moment too soon. It was still a very difficult event, both physically and mentally, for all of us. My weight dropped at one point to 143 lbs and Brad said he lost at least 20 lbs. But I was confident in the fact that I knew if we could continue to focus we would make it..."

Sincerely,

Lucian

After you ask and answer the first question of where you end and nature begins, the question on the heels of that answer is how you would like to be remembered. For me I believe that it should not be first and foremost that we all lived in big beautiful homes and we bought a lot of stuff, but instead we should be remembered as having not been afraid to speak up about issues that matter and that we cared enough to make sacrifices if necessary to right the wrongs. It was evident from those we met during this ride, that our actions will be the lead that others will follow, and that you lead first by doing and with this in mind, I am hopeful that this story will act as an inspiration to others to act and to lead in their own way and at their own pace, but in unison and soon.

CHAPTER TEN:
OUR FUTURE ENVIRONMENT:
A RIDDLE AND AN ANSWER

ABOVE Our spaceship Earth, with 7 billion people and billions upon billions of plants and animals on board, is a beautiful planet that is suspended in space and supported by a unique life support system of oxygen, water, and food; it is both resilient and fragile at the same time.

BELOW and OPPOSITE Our new technologies, when combined with our expanding human population, may have unplanned consequences. For example, Hoover Dam can store and provide water for millions across the west, but when we divert this water for human use without considering the needs of the natural systems, the water may no longer reach the sea – and the animals and plants that live in the Sea of Cortez, and rely on freshwater from the Colorado, are lost forever. On the other hand, White's Mill in Athens Ohio, on the Hocking River, has had minimal environmental impact but significant economic impact for generations, as the mill served farmers in the area and provided some power to homes and businesses close to the mill.

What do we know for sure? We know that the future will be different from today. We know this because today is already different from yesterday. We can count on this. Change is occurring rapidly, and technology is the driving force behind this. Technology is a double-edged sword, and what we can quickly change with positive results can also be altered in an ecologically negative manner as well. The rapid change brought about by technology, the speed at which it is occurring and the resulting impact—this is our dilemma.

The impact can be seen, for example, in a comparison between the impact that a local mill on a small river or stream in the early 1900s had on the ecosystem, in contrast with the global or regional impact large hydroelectric dam projects now have on Brazil or even on the western United States just 60 years later.

We know for certain that there has not been a day in the last four and a half billion years that the earth has not undergone change. We also know that humans, unlike other organisms, have consciously been able to alter and modify the environment. Our inclination to do so has grown dramatically over the last century and more specifically, within the last two generations. Technology has given us this power. With it, we can adapt and modify the environment as we see fit. We are learning, however, that technology cuts both ways.

Physicist Albert Schweitzer once said, "As we acquire knowledge, things do not become comprehensible, but more mysterious." Today I often hear that we are the most educated generation. If so, why are we not able to understand, acknowledge, or accept the critically important connection we have with the environmental tragedies we read about?

To many, our natural world remains a mystery. We have become a complicated society, and when we refer to our quality of life we concern ourselves with education, the arts, the homeless, AIDS, cancer and a host of worries and wants.

In the near term, in order to cope with our immediate demands, we will have to make small changes—in essence, plug the dike so that we can bring under control quickly the most threatening activities to our environment. To do this will require patience, compromise, cooperation and sacrifice. We have a host of wants and needs that society imposes on us today. For our near future, we need to find a balance. To do this, we should quickly identify those activities that represent the biggest threat, prioritize them, and then throw the majority of our resources, technology, money, and expertise behind them.

Our challenge now is three-fold.

First, we must, as individuals, bring that extremely important interrelationship—the balance of nature—back into focus. We must understand that we human beings play the most important role in doing so. Real knowledge is our most powerful tool. If we can help other individuals come to environmentally sound conclusions on their own, we will have made major progress. The logic and intuition we use in reaching these conclusions will continue to motivate us to act.

Second, we must focus on the pending marriage between the economy and the environment. They need to be one and the same, now and forever. In the last 35 years, our society has had the benefit of unprecedented growth and prosperity. It now appears that our rise in economic well-being has brought on a host of social and economic problems. We can no longer say that further growth will solve our problems. Quite the contrary, we can say that society is suffering the consequences of a growing economy.

We cannot say with certainty that all of our problems are the result of resource mismanagement, evil companies, greedy bureaucrats, uninformed politicians, and irresponsible special interest groups. Rather, they are a consequence of all of these factors and the decisions that were complicated by the constant "tug of war" of political, cultural, and economic tradeoffs along the way.

The most important role we can play is that of the consumer. If we make environmentally sound decisions in the market and cast our ballot for environmentally compatible products, the market will respond. If we simply do this, many of our environmental problems will be solved.

Finally, for our three-fold challenge, we need resolve and commitment to preserve, conserve and restore the balance. Preservation and conservation are two very different environmental terms. "Preservation" is a term that connotes protection from harm or damage. For example, preserving the Alaskan wilderness would require that people not be allowed to intervene, and that the area would remain pristine for years to come. "Conservation," on the other hand, implies that it is acceptable for us to manage our resources in a sustainable manner. But what is an appropriate use of a resource to one person may mean something entirely different to someone else.

In our society, the two terms are often contradictory. Simply put, we should preserve what we can when we can, and conserve what we can't preserve and restore what remains as best we can.

Our ecosystem is amazingly resilient. Given a chance, it will come back strong and vibrant, like the restored lakes we rode by in Ohio. Ecological restoration efforts are a more offensive approach, in contrast with the typical, more traditional defensive approach in both conservation and preservation. Restoration is a conscious attempt to compensate for our negative influence on the system. But we can undo that influence only when we understand it. To correct the harm we impose on our natural system, we must understand the precise nature of that imposition. And this presumes that we fully understand the system itself.

By committing ourselves to restoration, the cycle of influence and compensation, we obligate ourselves to seek a more exact understanding of our influence on the environment. This emerging "new understanding" will then have a positive effect on our future relationship with nature, and with the decisions we make.

With this in mind, it's vital that we aggressively embark on the road to restoration and discover many new and better alternatives.

PRESERVING, CONSERVING, AND RESTORING OUR ENVIRONMENT

Here are some of my thoughts on how we can go about preserving, conserving and restoring our environment.

The Rainforest

To understand the global impact of deforestation, we must first understand the basic biology of the rainforest and the causes of deforestation.

ABOVE Both temperate and tropical rainforests now cover less than 6 percent of the planet. Each day at least 160,000 acres (32,300 ha) of forest either disappear or are substantially degraded and along with them, we lose hundreds of species to extinction, the vast majority of which have never been documented by science. As these forests fall, more carbon is added to the atmosphere, which further contributes to global warming.

OPPOSITE While 25 percent of Western pharmaceuticals are derived from rainforest ingredients, less that 1 percent of these tropical trees and plants have been tested by scientists. The U.S. National Cancer Institute has identified 3,000 plants that are active against cancer cells, 70 percent of these plants are found in the rainforest. Vincristine, which comes from the rainforest periwinkle, has dramatically increased the survival rate for acute childhood leukemia since its discovery.

Rainforests cover less than 7 percent of the globe. They are predominantly found in a wet or moist band circling the globe along the equator. Tropical rainforests are some of the richest, oldest, most productive and genetically diverse ecosystems in the world. Between 40 and 50 percent of all living organisms (plants and animals) on this planet live in the rainforest.

What characterizes a rainforest? Temperature and rainfall. The equatorial rainforests, which represent about two-thirds of the world's rainforests, receive more than 250 inches of rain per year. The average temperature is 80 degrees Fahrenheit, with no seasonal fluctuation in temperature during the year.

The second main group of tropical rainforests receives less rainfall—40 to 160 inches per year—and has distinct wet and dry seasons. These seasonal rainforests are not as genetically diverse as the equatorial rainforests.

In years past, the rainforests covered over 14 percent of the earth's surface. Now they cover less than half of this. Most of the destruction has resulted from human intervention in the last 200 years, and more specifically since 1950. Of the remaining rainforests, almost 60 percent are located in Latin America.

Most people in developed countries are so far removed from nature they are unable or unwilling to perceive the relevance or relationship of rainforest organisms to their daily life. They do not know that many products they use come directly or indirectly from tropical rainforests. Some of the more common products are rubber, teak, mahogany, pesticides, medicinally useful drugs and many active anti-cancer compounds. Some food items include cashew nuts, avocado, mango, cocoa, coffee, and spices like vanilla and nutmeg.

We know that 25 percent of all prescription drugs marketed in the United States contain one or more rainforest plant compounds. We can assume that many new drugs are awaiting discovery in the rainforest, yet fewer than one percent of tropical species have been examined for their possible use by mankind.

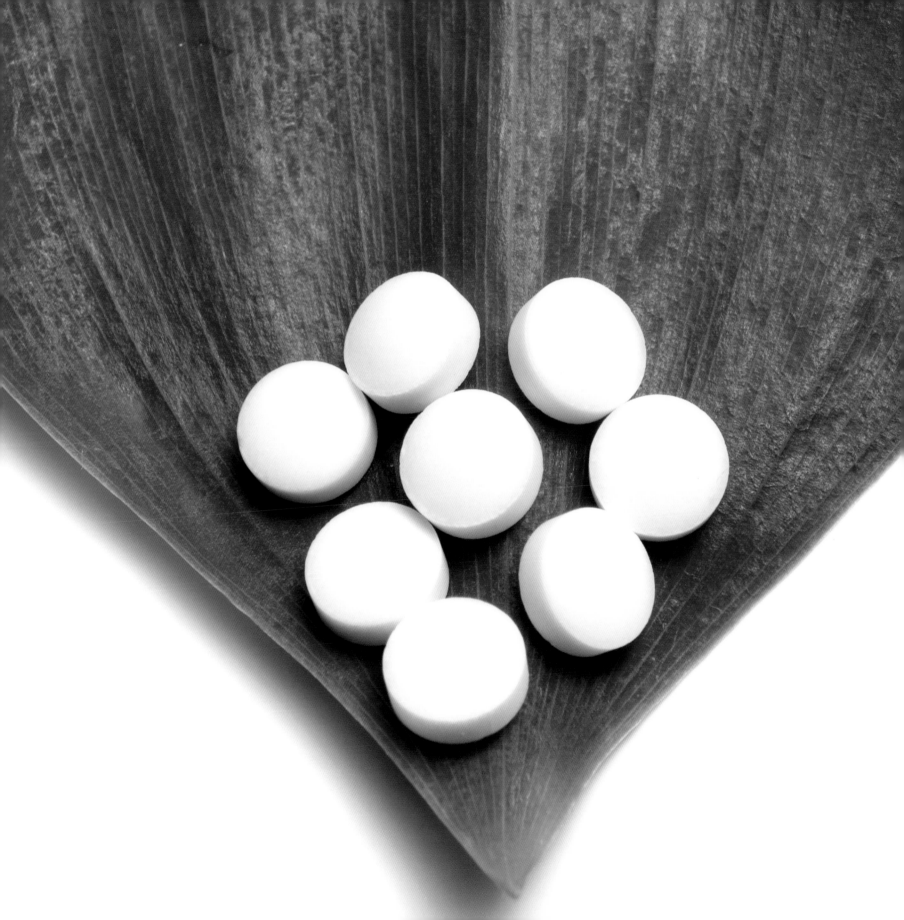

As deforestation continues, millions of yet undocumented and documented species of plants and animals go extinct. There are literally thousands, if not millions, of yet-to-be discovered species that could one day yield vital or economically valuable products.

"Deforestation" means the removal of large tracts of tropical forest for agricultural, urban, or industrial use. A "primary" or "virgin" forest is one that has been undisturbed for centuries. If it has not been disturbed, it is often called a "climax forest," which means it is no longer going through stages of development. Once primary forests are disturbed in any manner, they are no longer in equilibrium, and are now classified as "secondary forests." Human intervention is usually the cause.

Forest conservation implies that our use of the forest comes with a degree of preservation, and wise use of the forest involves trade-offs between preservation and development. The "gene pool" and "genetic diversity" refer to the quantity and variety of the individual organisms, populations, or species in the forest.

Tropical rainforests serve as a source of genetic material. It can, and currently does, provide products of economic and medicinal importance to people in both developing and developed countries. One example of why a gene bank is crucial can be seen in the Corn Blight of 1968. In the summer of that year, some farmers noticed a mysterious disease on their corn plants. This was the first sign of a very dangerous fungus that reproduced rapidly in the warm moist weather of 1968. Under these conditions, the disease spread across the Southeast, toward the United States' corn belt and proceeded to leave the cornfields in shambles.

This fungus, later called "The Southern Corn Leaf Blight," spread in four months from Georgia to Oklahoma. It spread so quickly because the United States corn crop was genetically uniform, so what affected one plant affected them all. For this reason, a diverse gene pool is very important.

Rainforests are being destroyed or severely degraded every minute of the day, every day of the week and every week of the year. The United States National Academy of Sciences reports that we lose an area the size of England, Scotland and Wales (50 million acres) each year. At this rate, we will lose all of the world's remaining rainforests by the year 2050, just forty years from now, and in turn, we will lose access to that genetic material forever.

What are the causes of this devastation? The four primary causes are: 1) commercial logging, 2) fuel wood gathering, 3) cattle ranching, and 4) small scale forest farming and population pressure. The causes are complicated, since they are simultaneously political, psychological and economical. Many people claim that the rainforests must be developed and conquered to help the poor and landless. In some cases, settlement of civilians by the government is meant to secure national borders by establishing a presence in the frontier region.

Some tropical forests are increasingly exploited because more people want more wood. The consumption of wood is expected to increase dramatically during the last years of this century. Of the total, one-third of the wood will be used as fuel in developing countries. Over

50 percent will be used in developed countries, where demand has been rapidly growing for construction products like plywood, veneer and particle board.

In Brazil, cattle ranching and subsistence farming have been the largest contributors to deforestation. Until the 1970s, the government sponsored a program that promoted colonization. The government gave ranchers incentives to exploit the rainforest and develop either farms or ranches. A large percentage of the clearing that took place was a result of various government incentives, but cattle ranching proved to be inefficient.

In many countries, meat production on a pound-per-acre basis is ten times what ranchers in Brazil will receive. Once the rainforest is cleared, the pasture or farm land has a life expectancy of less than eight years.

Conservationists have, in the past, boycotted the fast-food industry, and many restaurants now swear that they no longer use Latin American beef. However, this can be difficult to prove. Combination meat products are difficult to trace because once imported beef is inspected, it's allowed to enter the United States market without any requirement to show its country of origin.

As the demand in the West and Far East for cheap meat increases, more and more rainforests are destroyed to provide grazing land. Most of Central and Latin America's tropical and temperate rainforests have been lost to cattle operations to meet the world demand, and still the cattle operations continue as they creep southward into the heart of the rainforests.

Another factor contributing to deforestation is our booming world population. The largest percentage of this growth takes place in developing countries in rainforest regions. Small-scale forest (subsistence) farming, the search for fuel, and government programs to provide the landless poor with an opportunity to own property within the rainforest will, in the future, represent the largest threat to this ecosystem.

In the rainforest, the nutrients reside in the biomass, rather than the soil. The biomass is the total weight of all the organisms—plant and animal—in an area. The rainforest is so efficient and utilizes all of the nutrients so quickly that it's always in the process of transformation. Therefore, very few nutrients can be found in the rainforest soil. When a rainforest is burned, carbon is released as ash and briefly acts as a nutrient or fertilizer, allowing crops to grow. But as soon as this ash is used up, the soil becomes barren.

While the causes of the decline in rainforests are complicated, the role that rainforests serve in the global balance of nature is quite simple. As a gene bank, the rainforest, by supplying that genetic diversity, directly and indirectly protects all of the plants and animals on the globe, including the human population. These forests provide habitat for countless plant and animal species and they store massive amounts of carbon, which in turn, helps in the fight against global warming.

Studies have shown that the rainforest can produce natural products whose value far outweighs agricultural or ranching products.

The economic worth of these rainforests for purposes other than ranching and farming is significant and should be recognized.

If the present patterns continue, all or most of the world's remaining rainforest will be lost or severely degraded by the end of this century. When the trees are cleared away, little except scrub grass and weeds will grow in the poor soil. When plants and animals that used these trees for cover are exposed and die, the formerly lush forest will be replaced with a desert. This desert area tends to grow larger and creates a very dangerous spiral: with fewer trees, less vapor rises into the atmosphere, which causes less rainfall that in turn destroys more rainforest, and on and on.

Recognizing this, it's clear that preserving this belt of rainforest along the equator is one of the most important environmental stands that conservationists can take. The political implications of success here are as important as the biological consequences. If, through long-term sustainable development, environmentalists worldwide can influence the preservation of this fragile ecosystem, they will have won a battle of global significance.

What are some actions that we as individuals can take? Here are a few ideas to get started:

We can avoid eating fast food products that come from rainforest countries.
We need to read the label that specifies the country of origin of all food products.

We can avoid purchasing or using tropical wood products, and we can promote a local boycott of these products.

We can lobby our political representatives to support policies that reduce debt and promote sustainable management of resources in developing countries. These policies should tie aid in developing countries to environmentally appropriate land use and energy policy.

We can demand that producers provide alternative products. As consumers, we all place a demand on the market that the market will attempt to meet. Our demand acts as the driving force behind what we consume and produce. We must quickly become aware of that relationship and learn to harness this potential. Consumers must demand that producers provide alternative products.

The problems in America and other developed countries are linked to issues of too much, rather than too little. The ecology movement must become more linked to economic problems and less to ideology. I believe that ecological ideology has in general ignored the context of economic development from which the problems of pollution have been generated. We must bring the two closer together.

The Resilience of the Natural System—A Case Study

As I rode through Ohio and West Virginia, I encountered numerous streams that brought back memories of meandering hikes, fishing and swimming in this same area 15 years before. At that time, a popular swimming hole was Raccoon Creek, a small stream just 15 miles west of Athens, Ohio. At that time, our swimming hole had a big rope tied to a railroad trestle. The trestle crossed Raccoon Creek just before going into the Moonville Tunnel.

If you had the courage, you could walk out onto the trestle and jump off, or you could swing from the rope in a more exciting, but shorter fall. The trestle was at least 50 feet high, and the rope that swung out over the stream was probably 20 feet high at its apex.

Three things I will always remember about that swimming hole: 1) Even from the trestle, you could see the bottom of the creek. Before you took the big leap, you would always look first to see if any submerged debris were floating your way just below the surface, 2) the water was yellow-green, and 3) there were no fish living in the stream and very little plant growth.

My girlfriend, Kim, once said that she didn't want to swim in the stream because there might be fish that bite. I remember telling her that no fish lived in the stream so there was no need to worry.

The Rainforest Action Network's 1980s campaign against rainforest beef was largely successful in highlighting this problem. But today the problem continues as international demand for beef grows. Even though most of the ranchers operate at a loss, the ranchers' fortunes are made with government-subsidized loans, tax credits, and write-offs that come in return for developing the land. Beef production is a revenue stream but primarily a write-off and is only good for a few years as the lack of nutrients in the soil and overgrazing degrades the soil, the land is abandoned.

In most of the other lakes and streams in Ohio at that time, you couldn't see the bottom because of the proliferation of algae and other organisms that grew in the water. These were fertile, clean lakes and streams, and life grew as it should. But in Raccoon Creek and other area lakes and streams, the clarity of the water was not natural. Drain-off from strip mine pits or underground mines had seeped into the lake or stream and made the composition of the water uninhabitable for plant and animal life. In essence, these bodies of water were dead—great for swimming, but without life.

When I was in Athens during my ride, I drove out to Raccoon Creek. It was still there, along with the Moonville Tunnel, but the trestle had been dismantled. My younger brother, John, said that kids no longer went to Raccoon Creek but instead found other swimming holes. They now used a strip mine pit with the same symptoms as the stream: clear water and no natural plant and animal life. The symptoms persist—I took a look at the stream and found no evidence of improved water quality.

However, in another case, Lake Hope, a previously dead lake and another favorite swimming hole when I was younger, now offers swimming and boating and supports a very large population of bass and other game fish. By sealing the underground mines in the area and cleaning up and reclaiming many of the gob piles, the run-off of "yellow boy" and other residue into the lake has been reduced. The lake can now sustain normal plant and animal life. It's amazing how quickly that body of water rebounded.

What was essentially a dead lake 20 years ago is now teeming with life. This is one situation where strict environmental policy worked and the natural systems were able to rebound. There's still a lot of work that needs to be done in older mining areas, and further legislation will be necessary to strictly regulate the industry—but progress is being made.

The Environmental Movement

On the day the Los Angeles Lakers got their tails kicked by 34 points at the Garden (by Boston in game two of the 1985 series), Pat Riley told his team a quote his father had once passed on to him: "Somewhere, someplace, sometime you're going to have to plant your feet, take a stand and kick some tail."

Environmentally, I believe that time is now. We are involved in a dangerous experiment and must take a stand to gain control of our destiny. This will require that, as individuals and as a society, we must make certain sacrifices.

The technology already exists to clean up oil spills, develop alternative fuels, close the ozone hole, preserve the rainforests and stop or slow most environmental problems. But we must realize that we do not need to go out and invent new technologies to fix all our problems. We already know many of the answers, and we know what we need to do to correct not all, but many, of them.

OPPOSITE Some of the bleakest landscape in the U.S. can be found in Appalachia where miners have torn away the earth's surface to get at coal deposits. Using dynamite, bulldozers, and great earth movers, workers strip away the top soil to reach the coal seam that lies below, leaving land that is scarred and acidic. The acidic mine drainage that comes from these underground and strip mines makes its way into lakes and streams and the once-clear Appalachian streams are then contaminated by these exposed coal beds.

What we do not have yet is the collective political will and resolve to play out the trade-offs and make a concerted effort to set priorities so we can put the environmental issues at the top of the stack. Only when we do this can we channel our money, our technology, and our expertise into these problems and begin to see results. We need to do this as individuals first by changing our consumption patterns and the way we manage our lifestyles.

In parallel efforts, as the constituents of our elected leaders, we need to give these officials an environmental mandate. We must demand that our government approach these environmental issues on a more global level and coordinate with other countries to intervene on behalf of the environment. This mandate is very important and the trade-offs are many. When making a decision, our government will need to know that we have the resolve and the commitment to go the distance when it comes to these environmental issues.

We may not need to invent anything: we already have many of the tools we need, and many of the answers. Now, we need to focus on the problem and get others to cooperate.

The most significant aspect of the ride across America was the powerful emotional response that the environmental issue generated. This planet may be here during my generation and quite possibly the generation after mine, but will it be here for my grandchildren?

This is the first time in the history of mankind that we are not entirely certain the next generation, or the one after that, will have a home on this planet. It has always been our desire to pass on to our children a better society and a better environment, be it the family farm, better education, or less disease and war.

We are the first generation that won't be able to do this. Our children will instead be inheriting an over-used, hand-me-down planet that may be on its last legs and unable to support them and generations to come. What is frightening is that we have the power now to turn it all around—or not. If we don't, we have only ourselves to blame. We must rise to the occasion, take our lumps, and make whatever sacrifices are necessary to ensure that these natural systems survive and that we pass on to our children an ecosystem that can sustain generations in the years to come.

We must embrace the challenge and take control of our destiny. We all have an obligation to try and we all must try in our own way, I tried by riding a horse across the United States. Sting does it by having a concert, some do it by recycling, and others do it by simply reading this or other books and spreading the message.

The director of Friends of the Earth, Michael Clark, said at our first Ride Across America news conference that, "The most difficult thing to do is to explain to people the criticality of the problem without implying that it is too late and scaring them into doing nothing."

I agree, and I add: "Show people the problem and give them something to do." We must provide others with the opportunity to become involved and we can then give them hope.

Our ride was a way to attract attention to the issue and also to give many an opportunity to help. If we as individuals can provide an avenue of involvement, then this "Environmental

OPPOSITE Lake Hope is an example of a successful reclamation effort. At one point, the lake was exposed to acid mine runoff; as mining operations came to a close, reclamation efforts replaced topsoil and grasses to insure that the land surface was stable and resistant to soil erosion, which in turn allowed the lake to recover.

Movement" will continue to grow. The opportunity to get involved will become more and more important as the movement grows and interest builds because people with no way to help become frustrated. The challenge for people like those of us who are already involved is to help others make that same commitment. If we can find ways to enlist others in our efforts, we can keep this ball rolling.

It is not too late—far from it. This is the decade that will set the stage for years to come. The ecosystem is amazingly resilient, and with help it can bounce back, like the Lake Hope situation in Ohio. However, the ecosystem's response to the changes we have imposed upon it is much slower than the rate at which we are imposing those changes. We need to let the ecosystem catch its breath so we can cross the finish line together.

Already, we can see progress in many places. For instance, the recovery of lakes and rivers across the United States is encouraging; on a global level, developed countries recently committed to improving economic conditions through loans and grants for environmental problems in developing countries; there is phenomenal growth of membership in environmental groups, and finally, there is a greater global movement to pursue lower carbon energy sources.

The environmental havoc we have created on this finite planet may, in an unplanned twist of fate, be a blessing in disguise. Many would say that we are "up against the wall" environmentally. If so, the desperation we feel may force us to join hands in a global effort to clean up the mess. This cooperation may reduce global tensions and allow us to focus on common ground, rather than economic and political differences.

When the environmental movement began to emerge in the late 1960s, the members were willing to go to great lengths to challenge business policy. This approach seemed to justify itself as an attempt to bring attention to the new issue. The doomsday predictions and radical approach of the '60s, however, went over poorly with the business community and the response was a hard line against it. Over the next five decades, values, needs, and demands, combined with the ebb and flow of crises and attitudes on both sides, have brought on a mellowing, a sense of accommodation and maturing on both sides.

Yet, in spite of this progress, controversy, conflict and misunderstandings continue to exist as both sides continue to voice strong opinions. But at least there is the awareness that dialogue and compromise are essential for any real progress. It is apparent now to both sides that we need to find a reasonable blend that works: a sustainable economy and a safe environment.

Recently, changes in the economic structure in Europe and other parts of the world have caused business interests to think on a more global scale. Technology has made this a very small planet indeed, and has forced many in the business world to change their way of thinking. Changes in transportation now allow us to travel anywhere in the world in hours while advances in communication make it possible for us to communicate around the world while driving down the road in our cars.

Rachel Carson's *Silent Spring* ushered in a new era of environmental stewardship and awareness of our position and impact on the food chain, which in turn helped foster the legislation that resulted in the formation of the Environmental Protection Agency.

Because we are no longer isolated from one another, activities (economic, environmental, social, and cultural) in one part of the world can have an immediate impact in far flung reaches of the planet. A decade ago, it was commonly thought that resources, technology, labor, land, air and water were virtually infinite. The typical corporate horizon was short-term (quarterly, or at most a few years) and regional.

This viewpoint was in conflict with the ecologist's long-term, global and generational view of the world in which we live. This situation creates a dilemma, while the global community is a global market and economic opportunity it is also a global village with individuals who may not yet know how to live like neighbors.

It is clear that the methods are now here to bring us closer together. What we need now is the capacity to foresee the problems and then generate the new attitudes of accommodation that these rapid advances in technology require of us.

If it is true that when cultures differ, it will be harder for them to understand one another, it is also true that the more people differ, the more they have to teach and learn from one another. Today, as we move with lightning speed toward a true global community, most business people and environmentalists agree that we need a sustainable global economy that sustains an environmentally safe place in which to live.

For the first time, by and large out of necessity, this agreement is more than just rhetoric, and that is a significant step in the right direction. The market does not always reflect the true costs borne by society for current environmental and economic decisions. But we will eventually pay the piper—if not now, then in the future.

The 2010 summit in Copenhagen was termed the "Climate Change Summit." Happily, there was a consensus among the participating countries that further economic progress depends on improving world-wide environmental conditions. However, the results from this summit were overshadowed by the global economic crisis. As a result, only a limited accord was signed. Fortunately, the Cancun Summit that followed played out well and now we have agreements in place that can be translated into a UN process to advance the needs of our natural systems. In parallel support, environmental awareness is beginning to surface in developing countries. This is all very encouraging news!

In other ways, individual consumers have an impact. We can make environmentally sound investment decisions. As shareholders in both large and small companies, we have a voice and can require that our companies choose environmentally sound approaches to production and the business of doing business. Various money management firms have established socially responsible funds that guarantee our investments will be used in a socially and environmentally responsible manner. These funds require that companies address the effects of their business on society and the environment.

The poet Wendell Berry once said: "How superficial and foolish we would be to think that we could correct what is wrong merely by tinkering with the institutional machinery. The changes that are required are fundamental changes in the way we live."

We know, of course, that living implies that we consume. A result of this consumption is some level of waste. As society goes about the business of producing goods and services for the market, its activities are not 100 percent efficient. Production of goods and services and waste go hand in hand. Waste is often a result of production. The market plays a very active role in our economy and, as a result, of the production-waste relationship; it plays a very active role in the environmental arena, as well.

We realize that there is no way to make the waste from production and consumption and society, in general, go away. However, we can alter the amount, the manner in which it is introduced, and possibly even increase the ecosystem's capacity to absorb or assimilate the waste to minimize the pending impact. The problem is not to eliminate waste, but to learn to reduce, manage, or cope with a level that does not overwhelm nature's ability to assimilate and process that waste.

While the choice we must make is very clear, the decision to change our behavior and embark down this new road will be difficult. Because when I refer to *we,* I am referring to the collective *we,* and therein lies the problem. Even though it seems crazy to imagine that as intelligent as we are, we are incapable of making a conscious decision to act in global consensus, change our behavior and rise to this challenge. But this is actually the dilemma we are now facing. It is not whether we have the tools and technology to reverse the problems—because we do have the tools, technology and intellectual wherewithal to reverse the decline—the question now is do we have the resolve, commitment, and collective political will? The most often asked question on the ride was, "Can we turn this situation around?"

My reply was, "Can you?"

I know that in many cases the damage worldwide is significant, but at the same time I've seen the resilience of these natural systems. I am confident that we can work with these natural systems to significantly reduce the damage and lessen the long-term impact of our earlier mistakes.

I did not cross the United States by myself. I had a lot of help. Cooperation, compromise and the opportunity to become involved and aware were the keys to our successful ride. These same keys will help us restore the balance and integrity of our natural ecosystem.

Making this happen is more than a goal for each and every one of us. It's an imperative for the survival of our planet—and that of everything we hold dear.

This is a race that needs every rider possible—we're in it for "The Long Ride" and we're in it to win, so saddle up and ride like you never rode before.
Time's a wastin'.

OPPOSITE Lucian on a training ride, with his endurance horse Masquerade, in the desert at the base of the McDowell Mountains in Scottsdale, Arizona.

EPILOGUE

I began this book describing what it was like growing up as a young boy in southern Ohio, surrounded by nature. Those experiences forty years ago rewarded me with a unique appreciation of both the fragility and strength of Nature's systems. They also brought home to me the role we can play to right the wrongs we've made, and support, restore, and protect these natural systems.

Imagine fast-forwarding to the year 2031, as I have done so many times since I had my worst nightmare. Imagine having a brief, yet uncomfortable conversation with your children's children who are living in a world that can't reward them with a brilliant sunset, fireflies on a hot summer evening, fall colors, or the changing of the seasons when brown becomes green and then brown again.

What will those children say when we describe how it used to be, especially since they'll have no point of reference for what we are trying to describe?

Our planet records how we're treating it every day, like pages etched in the glaciers and the sediment that lies beneath our feet. These "pages" include the environment we humans are building on this planet, the growing number of genetically modified organisms that we develop with reckless abandon, and finally, the changes that evolve from the voracious consumption of our growing population

All these make for a very heavy footprint.

Now, twenty-two years after our ride across America, it is very clear that the outcome is in the hands of the seven billion people that reside on this planet. Today, because there are so many of us, we can change our climate's fate by simply choosing not to consume all that stuff we don't really need. By creating less waste, we can begin to shape the direction our planet's healing will take.

This is a heavy burden, but it's one that goes with the unique situation we have created through our actions. With this in mind, let's write a new book—one that our children will be proud to read—one that will show them that when we were confronted with the challenge, we made tough decisions and did the right thing.

Before I go into the details of where we all ended up after the ride, let me touch on an important observation about the character of those I met during the ride, as well as those today who are working to resolve these various environmental issues. As you read about these people, watch their careers, and learn about their commitment, you will be moved by their steadfast nature and their tenacity. And that goes for the horses, too!

I've found that this mix of commitment and tenacity is apparent in those who came on board early and are still working today on the same issues. Their passion is tinged with a sense of urgency and stems from a deep connection to the natural world. It's a commitment that's as natural as breathing…and I am so lucky that I had an opportunity to meet, work with, and learn from them all.

Where are they now?

It all started with **Bazy Tankersley.** Many of you may not know she is the creator and chief motivator behind the world-renowned Al-Marah Arabian breeding program. Her influence in the Arabian industry is legendary and her Al-Marah ranch is home to the oldest privately owned herd of Arabian horses in the world, its roots going back more than 200 years.

Her uncle, Colonel McCormick, ran the Tribune Company newspapers and her great-uncle invented the grain harvesting system, "the McCormick Reaper." Her mother was the first congresswoman elected from Illinois. Given this background, it should come as no surprise that when Bazy agreed to do something, it was as good as done. When she agreed to support our efforts and got on board first, her commitment and credibility brought us sponsors, horse enthusiasts, and other board members and endurance experts—all of whom contributed to the success of this event.

But it all started with Bazy, whose belief in our team anchored our ride and ultimate success. She was instrumental in funding the ride, serving on the board, and acting as my mentor before, during, and after the ride. Even today, as we are finishing *The Long Ride,* her help on this book has been instrumental. When I was hemming and hawing about the title, Bazy weighed in with insightful suggestions and the title of the book came from that discussion.

After the ride, Bazy won accolades for the breeding of her versatile horses. In 1999, with her son, Mark Miller, and Tim Farley, son of *The Black Stallion* author Walter Farley, they started the Black Stallion Literacy Foundation. By 2009, this program had touched over 350,000 students nationwide. Today, she continues with her breeding program and philanthropic endeavors.

In 2010, she was chosen by the Arabian Association in their Centennial 100 Celebration as the fifth most influential and significant contributor to the Arabian breed in the world over the past 100 years. Bazy continues to be a teacher, friend, mentor, coach and visionary to many. Without her help, none of this would ever have happened.

Bazy Tankersley

Randy Hayes

Leslie Barclay

Randy Hayes was an inspiration from the start and got on board when no one else would. He advocated on our behalf at every turn. Randy went on to work in city government as President of the City of San Francisco Commission on the Environment and Director of Sustainability in the office of Oakland Mayor Jerry Brown.

Additionally, he worked at the International Forum on Globalization, a think tank on the global economy, based in San Francisco. He is currently serving on the board of directors for the Rainforest Action Network and also directs the U.S. Liaison Office for the World Future Council based in Hamburg.

I reconnected with Randy in 2010 as I was winding up writing this book. As always, he jumped right in and lent a hand as a sounding board. We brainstormed through the complex logistics of bringing this story to life 22 years later.

If you were to mention the name **Ted Danson** back in 1989, when he helped us kick off our event, the long-running TV series, *Cheers,* would come to mind. What you may not know is that, besides being a well-known actor, Ted Danson has for the last 20-plus years consistently advocated the preservation of the ocean's ecosystem.

When I first met Ted, he graciously agreed to help us kick off our event by headlining a press conference in Tucson at Al-Marah Arabians. Now, over twenty years later, he continues to pursue a parallel path both as an actor and an environmentalist. After forming the American Oceans Campaign (AOC) in 1987 with his friend, Bob Sullnick, he continued to promote and advocate for this issue. Then, in 2001, the AOC joined forces with some other environmental groups to form what is now known as OCEANA. This organization is now the largest organization with the singular focus of ocean preservation and support. Ted serves on the board and just capped a career in environmental advocacy with his recent work as an author when he published *Oceana: Our Endangered Oceans and What We Can Do to Save Them.*

Leslie Barclay was instrumental throughout the event and hosted several fund-raisers. She served on the board for the ride, acted as a sounding board and event board member, and continued after the ride as an advocate and donor on a variety of environmental projects in Santa Fe, New Mexico. I spoke to Leslie in 1993 when she was involved in an effort to install a lagoon system on her ranch for treating effluent. Later that year, Leslie founded the Earth Works Institute in an effort to help develop, teach, and implement effective methods of land stewardship to protect the natural resources of this high desert region.

Since 1993, EWI has created demonstration models and education programs of sustainable food production, soil conservation, water harvesting, natural home design, forest and grassland management, and biological septic waste treatment. Leslie has inspired a legion of people to follow in her footsteps and pursue careers as stewards of the earth. Currently, she lives at Round the Bend Farm on the southern coast of Massachusetts, where she is involved in the production and sale of vegetables and meat for "locavores" (those who eat locally grown food), in partnership with a group of friends.

With the help of pigs, sheep, cattle, goats and chickens, the pastures are enriched and maintained by rotational grazing. Their manure provides a source of fertilizer for the vegetable gardens as well. The careful maintenance of woodlots sustains homes for numerous bird and animal species and affords summer shade for animals while functioning as a carbon sink. Leslie continues to serve on the Board of Directors of Earth Works Institute from her home in Massachusetts.

My business partners **Luis Lugo** and **Joe Tooker**, who supported my efforts during the ride, are respectively working in Sonora, Mexico and Kathleen, Georgia. After the ride, Luis became interested in environmental technology and went on to manage the Global Seawater implementation of saltwater farming along the coast of the Sea of Cortez while Joe stayed for a while in the IT field in Tucson and then moved to Georgia and went into senior management with a software company. Despite the ride's impact on our business, they backed my decision to continue and I am, to this day, appreciative of their support.

Lane Larson, a sounding board and mentor in my earlier years as we trekked and kayaked our way around the world, went on to become a renowned kayak guide. He led some of the most exciting expeditions to some of the most remote places on the planet. Lane and I met in Mexico for numerous dives in the Sea of Cortez after the ride and into the later '90s. He was considered one of the foremost authorities on the Sea of Cortez, and published numerous articles on the indigenous species that still inhabit some of the more remote islands in the northern Sea of Cortez.

Throughout the '90s, I joined Lane on many of his expeditions to these islands and dive sites. In his time, Lane was among the top river runners and whitewater-rafting expedition leaders in the world. He rafted three remote Alaska rivers sight unseen, and I was with him on his first trip down several rivers in Mexico. Every time he made it look easy.

In 2007, Lane died unexpectedly at his home in Tucson. This friend and mentor is still missed by those who knew him.

Bob and Bea Shepard masterminded the snakeskin rotation during the ride and handled many of the logistics. They retired as photographers and now live in Connecticut in the summer and Central America in the winter. They still have their Kachina doll collection and they still enjoy video photography.

The Ride Across America was an important chapter in "Bob & Bea's Great Adventure" as they traveled the United States, Canada, and Mexico in their Winnebago motor home from February, 1988 thru October, 1992. After the ride they returned to their home in Guilford, Connecticut for a few months before heading back out on the road. They visited Brad and Joyce's family in Texas in 1990, and that friendship endures today.

Bob continued to develop their video production company and Bea developed a career as an administrator for the association of Realtors, from which she retired in September, 2008. Bob and Bea are currently spending their winters in Sosua, Dominican Republic. They

ABOVE TOP Luis Lugo

ABOVE CENTER Lane and Wanda Larson

ABOVE Bob and Bea Shepard

ABOVE TOP Brad Braden

ABOVE CENTER Cassie Williams on March Along

ABOVE Wyatt La Fave on Sea Ruler

are involved in efforts to bring safe drinking water to the country through the use of bio-sand water filters. They are using their background and experience to help develop OlaTV, a fledgling local cable TV channel.

As I was searching for some of the photos from the ride, I made my first call to Bob. As luck would have it, he could provide originals for many of the photos. Not only had they collaborated with me on *The Long Ride,* they were instrumental in resurrecting many of the scenes from their memories, and from their notes and journals.

Brad and Joyce Braden returned to their home in Texas after the ride. They worked together for a time training horses with their son, Travis, and we kept in touch for a few years. I was saddened to learn in 1991 that Joyce lost her fight with cancer just after the first *Ride Across America* book was published. After Joyce's passing, Brad moved to Sedona, Arizona and worked on a small horse farm, training and breaking roping horses.

In 1994 at the age of 76, Brad returned to Crowley, Texas to work with Travis at the new Braden Training Center which opened in 1993. Brad continued as a horse trainer with his son and daughter-in-law, Kathleen, for many years. He passed away in June of 2009 at the age of 92.

Many of the scenes for this book were resurrected from notes and journals that Bea and Joyce kept on the ride. Their invaluable recollections and perspectives are peppered throughout this book, and they were very useful as I compared my notes and journal comments with their perspectives on the same events. I will be sending a copy of this book to Travis in Texas and also a copy of the notes from Joyce's journal of the ride.

Sweet William, Sea Ruler, and March Along

As you know from the book, **Sweet William** retired from the ride in Oklahoma and returned to Al-Marah in Tucson. Sweet William did it all—he went 1,440 miles and we trained another 1,000 miles prior to the ride. We rode day and night, day after day with no rest, state after state and he never faltered once. He was always ready to go the next morning.

After a short rest, he was recruited as a hunter jumper for awhile until Phyllis Robbins purchased him in 1995 as a trail horse. He served her for many years, carrying Phyllis and her friends on trail rides through the Santa Catalina Mountains.

In 2010, I got a Facebook email from a man in Tucson who managed the Redington Ranch Estates horse barn. It seems that Sweet William was retired and living out his years with a small herd of horses at Redington Ranch. His owner lived in Florida for the winter months but knew of Willy's past life as the lead horse on the Ride Across America.

The ranch manager contacted me and we set up a meeting to surprise Willy on his 29th birthday in October, 2010. He was doing very well and managed to voice a nicker when he saw me, probably because he thought I was bringing carrots. I gave him a big kiss and brushed him down a bit, which he thoroughly enjoyed. It was a beautiful morning in October and he lived on a beautiful ranch with a very nice ranch manager named George Kallas.

We took some pictures and we parted ways with the intent of coming back in a few months with a copy of the finished book for George and William to read together. But on March 22, 2011, Sweet Willy passed away at the age of 29. He was a great horse, and we will miss him dearly.

After the ride, Sea Ruler and March Along both returned to Al-Marah. Soon after, **March Along** was loaned out to a young lady named Cassie Williams, who lived in Oregon. "March," as we called him, was twelve years old in 1989 during the ride. When Cassie got him, she and March Along spent countless hours exploring the mountains of Oregon. Cassie grew up on March Along. She was seven years old when he arrived in her life and she spent days and weeks in the saddle. "March" took care of her and kept her safe.

He did the same for me on the ride, if you will recall, after Sweet William left the ride in Oklahoma. Whenever we got into a pinch, and I needed a steady unflustered mount to carry me through a difficult city, town, around the White House, mountains, rain, etc., we turned to March Along. He just had a way about him. He made sure he was always under you, and he was never flustered. He was a perfect horse for Cassie, who at seven was just learning to ride.

In 1998, he passed away. Cassie got another horse after March's passing but she told me as we were putting this book together that it was not the same. March was her first and best horse, and for us he was a steady member of our team. I am enclosing a note from Cassie that she wrote in 2011.

Sea Ruler also got a short rest and after a brief stint training as an endurance horse, he ended up just down the road from Al-Marah with Wendy La Fave, who worked with him as a pleasure and trail horse. She got Sea Ruler from Bazy's daughter Tiffany in 1994. The La Fave family rode Sea Ruler on the many trails in the mountain ranges surrounding Tucson, Arizona, including the Catalina, Tucson, and Rincon Mountains, as well as the Saguaro National Park. For the most part they would saddle up with his girlfriend and stall mate Mi Lady and they would head out the front gate into the surrounding desert and mountains. Sea Ruler quickly acquired the nickname George (short for Curious George) due to his mischievous yet sweet nature. He was a source of many smiles and lots of laughter as he roamed the yard knocking over, upturning, or munching on something not worth munching on. Wendy mentioned that her children Wyatt and Katherine rode him in the desert and around the family farm and they even had a blind friend in the saddle a few times. Wendy said they could walk away and trust that the kids were okay and in good hands around Sea Ruler. Sea Ruler was six when we did the ride and he was a young, playful troublemaker who would try to get March Along upset, just for fun. However, along the way on the ride across America, he started to mature and by the time we got to the East Coast, he'd become a very steady horse and trusted partner. Because of his high energy, I would do the long rides every other day on Sea Ruler. From Oklahoma to the East Coast, Sea Ruler did 70 percent of those miles while March Along did the balance.

"Hi Lucian,

My name is Cassie Jones (previously Cassie Williams). I was the lucky girl that Bazy Tankersley gave March Along to. I don't even know how to start to explain how much March Along meant to me and how much I love and miss him. As I write this, even though it has been 15 years since he passed, tears uncontrollably roll down my face. I was 7 when he was given to me. The 5 years that he was with me, March Along and I created a book of memories that warms my heart and makes me smile. He was such an amazing, beautiful horse. He was high spirited, loving and gentle.

Looking back I am still in awe of him and how he even took care of me. We lived in a tiny town named Jarbidge, Nevada that was located in a canyon. There were countless times I would take off on him down the dirt road all by myself. I usually rode bareback and all he had on was a halter. I would go catch him in the field, lead him up to a rock or fence so that I could climb on and we were off. He was not only fun to ride, but also sometimes my only mode of transportation. There were a few times I rode him to school!

When I was 11 we moved to Halfway, Oregon which was also a small town, though much bigger that Jarbidge. Halfway was also much more geared to Western style riding. After making a few friends I rode March Along to the local fairgrounds and we would all race around the track and barrel race in the arena. There was nothing March Along wouldn't do for me. I was happy to hear you were writing a book about your ride across the United States. I saw the pictures of March Along and I am proud of him.

Sincerely,

Cassie

ABOVE TOP Lori, Lucian, and Lauren with Dallas

ABOVE CENTER Lucian, Dorothy and John Spataro

ABOVE Lucian and Lucian Spataro Sr.

After talking with Wendy, it seems that his maturity and his high energy level served him well on their farm with numerous distractions. Sea Ruler was the mature horse that she put with her children, who would spend hours with him. He never tired of their games and attention. Sea Ruler died in March, 2009 at the age of 26.

My mother **Dorothy Spataro**, who for the duration of the ride accepted the task of watching over my house, mail and phone correspondence, buoyed our spirits with enthusiastic support and whose attention to detail was a big help, retired as a nurse and now lives with her Bichon puppy Precious in Tucson, Arizona. My father **Lucian Sr.**, who helped organize the Athens events and turned his home into a temporary ride stable and hotel and who also helped organize the events at the finish, has since retired from teaching as a professor and now lives with his wife Guang-zhen in Phoenix, Arizona. My brother **John Spataro** who was supportive and brought a sense of perspective to the ride, provided the theme song "A Horse with No Name" in the desert, and helped in Athens with his band and various horse activities, went on to graduate from the Roberto-Venn School of Luthiery and is now a custom guitar maker in Austin, Texas. My parents, whose example and outlook always encouraged me to explore, and through these somewhat circuitous explorations, I learned to not dwell on the perceived limits in life but instead to concentrate on the opportunities. Over time, these understandings and related experiences caused me to view each challenge as an opportunity, and for that and much more I am grateful.

Lucian Spataro Jr. returned to Ohio University after the ride to complete a Master's and Ph.D. in Environmental Studies. After concluding his studies, he returned to Mexico and in 1993, was named Vice Rector of Academic Affairs at the Universidad del Noroeste in Hermosillo, Sonora, Mexico. In 1996, he was appointed Director of the Academic Program on Sustainable Development at the University of Arizona's International College.

During this time, he authored numerous articles and publications on Sustainable Development and other environmental initiatives, and received numerous grants with the National Oceanic and Atmospheric Administration in that same area of research.

In 1999, he took a leave of absence from the University of Arizona and accepted an offer in the for-profit education arena to become Executive Vice President of the TesseracT Group. He was soon appointed President and CEO and asked to lead the restructuring of this publicly-traded education company (NASDQ: TSST). Lucian returned to the University of Arizona as a professor of Sustainable Development and simultaneously continued with his community-based educational endeavors and worked with Bazy and her son Mark Miller to start up the Black Stallion Literacy Project (BSLP) in Arizona. Ultimately, they were able to bring the BSLP to over 70,000 students in Arizona and then nationwide.

In 2006, he joined Anchor Management as Operations Officer, overseeing and working to improve the performance of Anchor's portfolio companies and providing interim management support. This firm serves the founders of Insight Enterprises (Fortune 500 NASDAQ: NSIT).

He is now serving as the Chief Operations Officer for Education2020, an education software company with headquarters in Scottsdale, Arizona.

Lucian continues with his equestrian and environmental interests and is now training and riding his endurance horse, Masquerade, a horse he got from Bazy in 2008. The horse, interestingly enough, could be a twin to March Along, Sweet William or Sea Ruler.

When Lucian got Masquerade, his subsequent riding and discussions with Bazy triggered his interest in writing *The Long Ride*. Now, three years later, Lucian is riding in various endurance events while work on the book comes to a close.

Lucian is also active in various preservation and educational projects in the McDowell Mountain Park, where he rides Masquerade near his home in Scottsdale, Arizona. He also works with the Sonoran Institute and its environmental restoration and educational efforts along the lower Colorado River and the Colorado River delta in Sonora, Mexico.

He calls Scottsdale home, where he lives in the shadow of the McDowell Mountains with his wife Lori, daughter Lauren, and their black lab Dallas and endurance horse Masquerade. He continues to write and speak on environmental and sustainable development issues to audiences from K-12 to college and to civic, business and environmental groups as well.

ABOVE Lucian and Masquerade training in the McDowell Mountain Park in 2010.

BELOW March Along in Oregon, backpacking with Cassie.

USEFUL INFORMATION

Al-Marah Arabians

Al-Marah is the vision, lifelong love and work of Bazy Tankersley, a luminary in the Arabian horse industry worldwide, and a dedicated shepherd of the breed.

4101 North Bear Canyon Road
Tucson, Arizona 85749
Phone: 520-749-1162

www.al-marah.com

Earth Works Institute (EWI)

EWI is a Santa Fe-based non-profit organization that helps communities grow toward economic resilience through environmental health. EWI pursues its campaign from the ground up, by empowering youth, mobilizing communities and facing climate change.

1413 South Second Street, Suite 4
Santa Fe, New Mexico 87505
Phone: 505-982-9806
info@earthworksinstitute.org

www.earthworksinstitute.org

Easy Care Inc., Easyboots

What began in 1970 with the invention of the Easyboot has since grown into a full line of hoof boots and natural hoof care products that protect the hoof and allow horses to cover rough terrain and aid in the treatment of hoof problems.

2300 East Vistoso Commerce Loop Road
Tucson, Arizona 85755

www.easycareinc.com

Fleeceworks

Manufactures of the world's finest Australian Merino Equestrian Products. We are riders and competitors, who are passionate about horses.

432 Maple Street, Suite 7
Ramona, California 92065
tel. 760.788 5949
fax. 760.788 5920
information@fleeceworks.com

www.fleeceworks.com

Green Rider

Publisher of The Long Ride *and sponsor of various environmental and equine events.*

c/o Lucian Spataro
PO Box 25223
Scottsdale, Arizona 85255
Phone: 480-570-6896
email: Lucian@thelongride.com

www.thelongride.com

How On Earth, The Store

How On Earth is an organization that seeks to reestablish the diverse agricultural use of our remaining farmlands and the vibrant economy that accompanies quality local food production.

62 Marion Road
Mattapoisett, Maryland 02739
Phone: 508-758-1341
email: thestore@howonearth.net

www.howonearth.net

Jane Goodall Institute

With Dr. Goodall's words and actions as inspiration, The Jane Goodall Institute advances the power of individuals to make informed decisions and take action to protect and improve the environment of all living things.

4245 North Fairfax Drive, Suite 600
Arlington, Virginia 22203
Phone: 703-682-9220

www.janegoodall.org

350.org

350.org is an international environmental organization that is building a grassroots movement to confront climate change and cut emissions to a level that is lower than 350ppm CO2 in an effort to slow the rate of global warming.

Phone: 510-250-7860

www.350.org

Oceana

Oceana works to protect and restore the world's oceans and is the largest international ocean conservation and advocacy organization.

1350 Connecticut Avenue, NW, 5th Floor
Washington, D.C. 20036
Phone: 202-833-3900
info@oceana.org

www.oceana.org

Ohio Valley Environmental Coalition (OVEC)

OVEC's mission is to organize and maintain a diverse grassroots organization dedicated to the improvement and preservation of the environment through education, grassroots organizing and coalition building, leadership development and media outreach.

PO Box 6753
Huntington, West Virginia 25773-6753
Phone: 304-522-0246

www.ohvec.org

Platinum Performance

Platinum Performance is a leading provider of the finest equine, canine, and human supplements and health education.

90 Thomas Road
PO Box 990
Buellton, California 93427
Phone: 800-553-2400

www.platinumperformance.com

Rainforest Action Network (RAN)

RAN campaigns for the forests, their inhabitants and the natural systems that sustain life by transforming the global marketplace through education, grassroots organizations, and non-violent direct action.

221 Pine Street, 5th Floor
San Francisco, California 94104
Phone: 415-398-4404
answers@ran.org

www.ran.org

Sonoran Institute

The Sonoran Institute, founded in 1990, works with communities in Western North America to conserve and restore unique natural landscapes, wildlife, and cultural values.

7650 East Broadway Boulevard, Suite 203
Tucson, Arizona 85710
Phone: 520-290-0828

www.sonoraninstitute.org

SPOT

The SPOT satellite GPS safety system makes leaving everything behind both a fun and safe adventure. If you are out riding your horse in the desert or in the mountains and you have an accident, you can use the SPOT to inform others of your situation and send help your way.

www.findmespot.com

World Future Council

The World Future Council operates to speak and advocate for policy solutions that serve the interests of future generations and acts as a voice for the needs and rights of future life.

660 Pennsylvania Avenue, SE Suite 302
Washington, D.C. 20003
Phone: 202-547-9359

www.worldfuturecouncil.org

Lucian and Sweet William on his
29th birthday in October, 2010.